PRAISE FOR
OF MARKETING

'Is your marketing failing? Study this book. Carlos Gil reveals a strategy for developing a loyal community in an age where loyalty is hard to come by.'
Michael Stelzner, Founder and CEO, Social Media Examiner

'Carlos Gil's illustrious career makes him expertly positioned to help readers navigate the ever-changing world of marketing technology. It's exciting to find a book that provides both a strategic roadmap as well as detailed common-sense advice. It's a must-read for both seasoned marketers and those who are just starting the journey to build a personal brand.'
Bonin Bough, Founder and Chief Growth Officer, Bonin Ventures

'Carlos Gil is relentless in his dedication to his craft. Don't bother reading *The End of Marketing* if you aren't ready to alter your stale marketing mindset.'
Leah Dorsey Harris, Content and Programming Director, Digital Summit Series

'Razor-sharp, insightful and unafraid to say it like it is. Carlos Gil paves the way for a new era in marketing.'
Gerard Adams, Co-founder, Elite Daily

'Carlos Gil is one of the most brilliant marketers I've ever had the pleasure of working with and his insights and knowledge are critical to succeeding in business today. *The End of Marketing* is essential reading for entrepreneurs and marketers alike. The author is right: marketing is dead; human connection and emotions are what drive people and their actions.'

Josh Machiz, Head of Client Engagement, Nasdaq

'I first saw Carlos Gil speak at SXSW in 2016 and immediately hired him to work with our company. His knowledge, expertise and ability to teach and or implement best practices puts him in an elite category.'

Chris Heller, Chief Real Estate Officer, OJO Labs

The End of Marketing

Humanizing your brand
in the age of social media and AI

Carlos Gil

KoganPage

Publisher's note

Every possible effort has been made to ensure that the information contained in this book is accurate at the time of going to press, and the publishers and author cannot accept responsibility for any errors or omissions, however caused. No responsibility for loss or damage occasioned to any person acting, or refraining from action, as a result of the material in this publication can be accepted by the editor, the publisher or the author.

First published in Great Britain and the United States in 2020 by Kogan Page Limited

2nd Floor, 45 Gee Street	122 W 27th St, 10th Floor	4737/23 Ansari Road
London	New York, NY 10001	Daryaganj
EC1V 3RS	USA	New Delhi 110002
United Kingdom		India

www.koganpage.com

ISBNs

Hardback	978 0 7494 9758 3
Paperback	978 0 7494 9757 6
Ebook	978 0 7494 9759 0

British Library Cataloguing-in-Publication Data

A CIP record for this book is available from the British Library.

Library of Congress Cataloging-in-Publication Data

A CIP record for this book is available from the Library of Congress.

Typeset by Integra Software Services, Pondicherry
Print production managed by Jellyfish
Printed and bound by CPI Group (UK) Ltd, Croydon, CR0 4YY

CONTENTS

About the author ix
Acknowledgements x
Foreword by Brian Solis xi

01 Marketing is dead 1
Know your audience – who are they and what channels
  are they on? 8
What value do you bring to your intended audience? 8
Who are your references? 8
Who has perceived influence among your target
  consumers and how can you align with them? 9
Create your own influence 10
References 16

02 Stranded in a digital ocean 17
Getting social media users to engage 20
Be where your customers are 23
Analyze what content works 26
Less promotion, more interaction 30
References 32

03 How to be savage AF – like Randy 33
Be likeable but be a savage 38
Finding your brand mentions 40
Finding your brand mentions alongside competitor
  brands 41
Finding your competition's mentions
  in specific contexts 42
Using industry mentions to find prospective
  customers 44

Monitoring reviews of your brand 45
Engaging with your competitors' social media ads 45
Strategies to change how your company is perceived
    on social media 46
References 51

04   **Don't be mad at Facebook; you just suck
      at marketing** 53
Don't hate Facebook – get better at marketing 56
Understanding Facebook's algorithm 58
Types of content to avoid posting on Facebook 61
How to growth hack your Facebook content 63
Create content that converts 66
Conducting an audit of your Facebook pages 67
References 70

05   **Swipe right: sales and marketing is no different
      from finding your match on Tinder** 71
The start of Snapchat 73
Don't overly rely on platforms 78
Living in a Tinder world 80
Carefully map out your story, aka 'storyboarding' 81
Write short one- or two-sentence captions 82
Ask open-ended questions to maximize engagement 83
Ditch stock photography and replace it with real-life
    user-generated moments 83
Marketing is like dating 84
Reference 87

06   **Growth hacking your way to greatness** 89
Cheating isn't winning 91
Growth hacking 92
Facebook Groups 100
LinkedIn Groups 101
Facebook Watch Party 102

Native blogging 103
How to frame content for maximum engagement 103
Create Instagram and Twitter pods 104
Automate engagement with bots 105

07   Marketing lessons from social media giants DJ Khaled and Kim Kardashian West 109
Five key points for social media success 116
Ten steps to telling the perfect story 119
Reference 124

08   Transforming your advocates into the faces of your brand 125
Why does employee advocacy really matter? 130
Getting buy-in throughout the company 131
Keys to successful employee advocacy program rollouts 134
How to keep up momentum after launching 136
References 142

09   Judgment day: the battle of AI versus humans 143
Machine learning 144
Predictive analytics 144
Artificial intelligence 145
The future is happening now 145
Buying 'fake' followers and 'fake' engagement 150
Following and unfollowing tactics 151
Auto-like and auto-comment 151
References 157

10   The power of personality and persuasion 159
Meet 'The 5Ps of Success' 161
Add rich media content 173
Update often and monitor 175

Join LinkedIn Groups 176
Find relevant groups 176
Introduce and engage 176
Create industry thought leadership 178
Create video content 179
Have a plan and be consistent 181
You can't post once a day and walk away 181
Each channel requires its own strategy 182
What to do in-between posts 182
Reference 184

11   Bringing it all together 185
How to hack the Facebook algorithm 188
Cracking the code on Instagram 189
Turn customers and employees into advocates 190
Have a strategy for each platform 192
Tools to use 192
FAQs 195
Above all, be social 204

12   The new frontier 205
Evolve or die 207
How to continue to engage new audiences 209
Millennials and the C-suite 211
The platforms 211
Final thoughts 212
The new marketing department 215
Create your influencers 216
Conversational marketing 217
Conclusion 217
References 219

Index 220

ABOUT THE AUTHOR

Carlos Gil is an international keynote speaker and award-winning digital storyteller with over a decade of experience leading social media strategy for global brands including LinkedIn, Winn-Dixie, Save-A-Lot and BMC Software. A first-generation Latino American, Gil's work has been featured by CNNMoney, *Harvard Business Review*, *Entrepreneur* and Social Media Examiner, in addition to dozens of trade publications. At present, Gil is the CEO and founder of Gil Media Co., a full-service digital marketing firm based in Los Angeles, which works with Fortune 500 clients.

ACKNOWLEDGEMENTS

First, to God be the glory for putting me in situations throughout my life, which made me who I am today. I wholeheartedly believe that we are a byproduct of our circumstances, including the people we meet and the situations we encounter along the way. While I am grateful for the mentor figures throughout my professional career who helped guide me during critical points of my adulthood, it's my parents that have always had my back since day one. Thank you to my mother, Millie Gil, for first introducing me to LinkedIn on one fateful day in November 2008. I often wonder where I'd be or who I'd be had I never took her advice to look into it. As they say, 'mom knows best'. To my father, Carlos J Gil, there are four pieces of advice that you've always shared with me that anyone reading my book should know: 1. The worst type of fear is the one you anticipate; 2. Always keep your lightbulb on; 3. Never discuss money, religion, or politics outside of your home; and 4. It's better to be the head of an ant than the tail of an elephant. Thank you for your wisdom, always, Dad. Lastly, thank you to Chris Cudmore, Lachean Humphreys and the entire team at Kogan Page for helping me bring this book to life and, more importantly, for believing in me. It was my goal to write a book, and I did it. Everything else from this point forward is a bonus. Thank you.

FOREWORD

This is the end of what was and the beginning of what's next

I've known Carlos for several years now. After years of building an online friendship, we finally met in person, ironically, during a digital event on the first floor of Twitter's headquarters in San Francisco. We immediately struck up a real-world friendship, one I enjoy to this day. I'd always respected Carlos's drive and 'real talk' approach to digital engagement. But more so, I grew to admire who he is as a person. The Carlos that I got to know over the years is genuine, thoughtful and caring – the kinds of qualities you want to see in everyone, everywhere, but are often rare. This is why we cherish these special qualities when we actually see them in others.

I guess that's what this is all about.

No matter what we do in life, whether personally or professionally, humanity counts for everything.

It's that authentic sincerity and consideration that forms the foundation for the most meaningful and mutually beneficial relationships. You know it when you feel it. Whether it's online or in the real world, this foundation defines the nature of our engagement and connection. But with digital comes an opportunity to strengthen these foundations to scale exponentially.

We're incredibly fortunate to live in a time when we have access to new genres of relationships and connections. When you think about it, we were given gifts to connect with people we wouldn't normally have seen or heard from otherwise. You too, were bestowed with gifts to reach others who would most likely never know your name or what it is that makes you... uniquely you. But more so, we were presented with incredible, rich new sources for fresh perspectives and ideas and unconventional ways of communicating, thinking and learning.

These gifts changed everything.

Media was socialized. Information, relationships and influence were broadly democratized. The world became much smaller and more accessible. Suddenly, everyone was given a voice, unforeseen promise and empowerment, and a chance to change the future. It's now possible for everyone to broadcast and consume media and interact with one another on demand... all day... all night... every day. And, we do. Maybe, too much.

Not everyone realizes the value of these gifts however.

For some, these precious gifts introduced dynamic means and capabilities to do the same old things as before, but in new places. They broadcast messages, talk rather than listen, promote instead of learn, and build audiences over communities.

The promise of these gifts is still largely untapped. The opportunity is there however, for anyone who can see possibilities in a new light, without the shackles of legacy perspectives or biases of past measures of success.

We now live in a time where people are becoming brands and brands are trying to become people. Yet somewhere along the way, we have all been guilty of exaggerating the 'me' in social media rather than perpetuate the humanity of what it means to truly be social.

As social and all forms of media become increasingly intelligent, the time is now to break free from mass conventions and our over-emphasis on shiny objects and finite trends. The gifts are still abundant to do so.

With the right perspective and intent, and with a little empathy added for good measure, emerging intelligent platforms can shine the spotlight on the people and the insights that matter most to us. With artificial intelligence (AI) though, ironically, we're offered a chance to become *more* human. But AI also carries with it the dangers of reinforcing dated biases to only make media ever more anti-social.

Everything changes with you.

That's the power you have and the potential you already possess.

The gifts before you and those on the horizon are not bound to any previous outlooks, practices or protocols. They're only limited by imagination, purpose and conviction.

You have a choice in what you do differently.

If there's any assurance I can offer, it's that most people will choose to follow what they already know. In doing so, they won't truly break new ground. They won't truly create new value. They won't sow more meaningful relationships.

Yet here you are faced with a future that is largely unwritten. What you do from this moment on will set you apart from the ordinary. Your path will offer new hope and lead to surprising and rewarding experiences. Your path will blaze a trail for others to follow.

Up to this point, I've made no mention of the word marketing. Herein lies the magic of the journey on which you're about to embark.

Historically, marketing hasn't been synonymous with relationships. This is after all about people, not just technology. Yes, it should have always been that way. So, it's up to you to change course. It's up to you to bring to life a bright and promising human-centered future.

Because of your vision and your work, we can put the social back in social media. As a result, people and relationships will benefit from the artful and personal coalescence between innovative technologies, empathy and mutual value.

That's the thing about endings… they always make way for new beginnings. And, this is yours. You are needed more than you may realize. Let's go…

Brian Solis

01
Marketing is dead

Marketing, as we know it, is dead.

Now, as you read this, you're probably saying to yourself: 'Yeah right, marketing isn't dead – it will never die'. But then, ask yourself a sincere question: When was the last time that you saw an ad – whether it was on TV or online – and immediately pulled out your credit card and made a purchase solely based on impulse? If you can't remember, it's because the likelihood of a single ad influencing you to convert to becoming a customer hasn't happened – ever.

However, I'd be willing to bet that in the last year or two you've probably been influenced to do one of the following:

- You purchased a pair of sneakers that your favorite celebrity wears... because you want to be perceived at work or by your internet friends as 'cool'.

- You downloaded a song on iTunes or Spotify that someone you follow on Instagram shared onto their Instagram Stories... and suddenly it's your favorite jam because everyone else is into it.

- You took a dream vacation to a popular destination because your go-to YouTube personality showed you what an amazing time they had at the resort where they stayed... and then you told anyone that would listen about the incredible experience you had.

- Let's not forget, it's likely you participated in the '10 Year Challenge', 'In My Feelings Challenge', 'Ice Bucket Challenge', 'Mannequin Challenge' or experimented with the Keto diet because everyone in your collective digital circles was doing it.

Am I right? If you answered 'yes' to any of the above, then you are the consumer that the company you work for is desperately trying to engage but is failing miserably to do so in the process. This isn't marketing anymore – it is psychology used as a tool to sell and monetize. And it works.

Call it 'fear of missing of missing out' (otherwise known as 'FOMO') but today's consumer wants to be part of something bigger than their everyday life. The reason why millions of people gravitate to social media every single day isn't necessarily because we are all extroverts and enjoy interacting with strangers, but instead it's to escape the realities of the ordinary lives we all live, stuck in-between a 9 to 5 job, kids, spouses and hobbies. The reason we watch reality TV is the same reason we subscribe and opt in to follow digital influencers and celebrities – it's to escape reality. Social media doesn't just connect us to people, it connects us all to a parallel universe where we are suddenly more popular, have more friends and have voices that travel outside of our communities and cities.

As of March 2019, 56.3 per cent of the world's population has internet access – that's an estimated 4.3 billion people who have access to a world that primarily exists on a cell phone or computer (Internet World Stats, 2019). With the size of this online community, the internet today isn't just a place to shop or research. Unlike other forms of mass media like TV, radio and newspapers where the communication primarily flows from one to many, the internet – and social media in particular – naturally facilitates multiway communication, providing an interactive place to chat about celebrity gossip and politics, rant and rave about our favorite sporting events and awards shows, or react to brand campaigns and social movements like #MeToo.

Because of the way social media facilitates multiple forms of communication including one-to-one and many-to-many, consumers today instinctively only care about your latest ad campaign if their friends are also speaking about it. These conversations might start online and then flow to offline communication, which can then fuel more online conversations.

Since communication has shifted, marketing must too. The reason why some marketing professionals are pessimistic about social media is that you can't advertise and sell to consumers the same way that you would historically have run a print or TV ad. In the 'old days', pre-social media, iconic brands like Nike, Coca-Cola and others didn't have to do much to convince the masses to buy from them. They either showed up on your TV or in a magazine with their globally recognized logo, a celebrity figurehead endorsing them and a catchy slogan that an advertising agency came up with, and you had lightning in a bottle.

Today, marketing and advertising require a new way of thinking and an understanding that the digital landscape is built on genuine communication instead of mass communication. To that point, consumers today don't want to be sold to – they want to be engaged and be a part of a movement. Your challenge isn't 'how to market' to your target consumer; instead, your objective should be how do you engage your target demographic to become an advocate for your brand and in return have them convince their friends to join.

The good news is that this form of scaling your message shouldn't be entirely new to marketers: it's similar in principle from messaging in the 1980s and 1990s, such as teenagers showing off their latest clothes and sneakers to friends at the mall, thereby encouraging a wider group to buy more.

But merely having a recognizable logo doesn't cut it anymore. Thanks to technology, those days are behind us. The shopping mall arcade and food court aren't the cool, hip places to hang out anymore. Now, it's a *Fortnite* group online party whereby teenage kids like my son are dropping mom and dad's credit card to ensure that their character is perceivably cooler than their friends'. According to its developer Epic Games, *Fortnite* grew to over 125 million players from 2017 to 2018 (The Fortnite Team, 2018). Yet when you run a quick search on Twitter for 'Fortnite' there's a noticeable lack of companies interjecting their brand into a conversation among a community of gamers that attracts over 40 million players per month.

If you're McDonald's, PepsiCo or a brand that appeals to teen-agers or young adults, tapping into this audience is as easy as creating an account on Twitch, branded by your company and inviting micro-influencers, in this case the gamers, to play on your account. You could then cross-promote on your Facebook page, Instagram account, Twitter channel and email list.

It's that easy, but so far, it's not being done. What is disappointing about this is the lack of awareness that comes from the C-level at many companies, which seem to choose to think of social media as a secondary or even tertiary medium for marketing and advertising. Most major corporations employ dozens of highly educated, annual six-figure earners to work in their marketing departments, yet by not tapping into the potential of social media, they're not getting the most out of their employees.

That disconnect is because, often, we fail to separate who we are as consumers from who we are as professionals. What we want as consumers often doesn't align with what we expect as marketers from our customers. Meanwhile, there is a 16-year-old kid somewhere in the world right now who's making six figures per month with an Instagram meme account or a Shopify or Amazon store drop-shipping products like t-shirts and nutritional supplements without owning a single printing press or warehouse.

While marketing as we know it is dead, clearly consumerism is very much alive and well. People will always need goods, products and services. Even when cars become autonomous, we will always need vehicles and transportation no differently to how we will still need clothing to wear, places to visit and people to see. Because we are not robots – we are humans.

And as humans, we all feel a need to be acknowledged, wanted and loved. As such, brands need to do a better job making customers feel valued, and that requires understanding who your target customers are and where to connect with them.

Whether you are a service provider, a talent who is hungry for work or a brand itself, social media makes it easy to find and directly connect with customers. Imagine being able to go to Google right now and type 'Find customers who are looking to buy XX' and seeing real-time search results. It already exists. By tapping into Twitter or Instagram as search engines, you can run searches to find your ideal audience.

But before you start implementing these strategies and using social media to its fullest potential, it's important to first understand the ethos behind why it can work so effectively. It's a challenging notion, and one that can be difficult to implement. And this is the notion I want to convey to you:

> People don't buy from logos, they buy from people.
> People trust people.

We are living in a new era whereby people have the power to influence the masses from an iPhone anywhere in the world. The game of marketing is no longer played exclusively by billion-dollar corporations.

However, if you want to win the game, you need to make people – not your logo – the face of your brand. The reason I have dedicated over a decade to educating professionals about the power of social media is that I believe in it as a result of what social media has meant to me, both personally and professionally.

In 2008, I was laid off from the banking industry due to the economic recession in the United States. In spite of my layoff, social media was a catalyst in helping me rebuild my career and a network of connections that are invaluable. It's through social media, and countless hours devoted to studying 'the game', that I learned how to grow a business during the economic recession with no marketing budget.

As a result of my efforts over that period, I later went to work for corporations, including LinkedIn, where I was responsible for leading social media teams and thus was tasked with convincing company executives at every brand where I worked why social media is essential.

I know what it's like to be a team of one and be continuously turned down because my superiors don't understand the value in it, but I can also tell you that the data doesn't lie. And you can find more data today on consumer behavior than at any point in human history.

Fast-forward to today: every day I'm approached – whether it's in person at a conference or privately through Facebook Messenger – by professionals who are still trying to make sense out of tools that aren't new, but are always evolving. My answer to them is always first to understand the fundamental ethos: less selling, more listening and engaging.

I believe wholeheartedly that as Baby Boomers and Generation X become supplanted by Millennials and Generation Z as the primary economic drivers of global consumerism, that if brands want to survive – and thrive – through the next industrial revolution, then they need to find a way to personify who they are and step from behind the digital curtain. Going forward, Coca-Cola will need to be a person that I can relate to. A real face that personifies the brand and convinces me to buy Coke instead of Pepsi. Nike will need to be a team of athletes that I and others should aspire to be like. Whole Foods will need to be a series of people who teach me how to make better choices in how I eat. Delta will need to be people who show me the world through the lens of their camera. My local gym will need to be a person who teaches me how to work out.

The fact is, for every fitness influencer, for every beauty blogger, for every travel influencer that exists, that is one more person who is taking market share away from your company. You are competing for digital reach with the same influencers that you are temporarily hiring to endorse your brand. And this model doesn't work.

This isn't the 1990s anymore. Snoop Dogg and Dr. Dre aren't telling the teenage version of you to head over to Sam Goody to pick up their latest CD. Instead, Drake is convincing every 13- to 35-year-old to download his music by giving you an intimate glimpse of his life on Instagram while Taylor Swift can be found chatting with fans on Twitter. If you had said to me when I was a kid that one day there would be no ToysRUs and that Nintendo would be less popular than the brand that made the Walkman (Sony) I would've said you were insane.

This is a New World Order... of business. You only have to look as far as AOL and MySpace to see what happens when your audience grows up and you don't grow up with it.

Thanks to technology, consumers are the media. Today, with an iPhone and an Instagram account, every person is an influencer. This is part of the reason why brands, and the marketers behind them, don't buy into social media: because brand is no longer superior to the consumer in the eyes of the consumer. It's about control – but it shouldn't be. Of course, you can't control what people say about you – but you can steer the conversation in the direction that you desire, should you choose to engage and be a part of it. That's the key – brands should be aiming to be a part of the movement, and avoid falling into the trap of trying to be the movement itself. To a certain extent, control has been relinquished not to the entity that has the most marketing budget to spend but rather to the people whose message goes the furthest.

Brands shouldn't view these platforms as their biggest enemy. They are also your biggest ally, and today, one that you cannot live without. Facebook is one of the most – if not the most – powerful corporations on the planet. Mark Zuckerberg and company have transformed the way that we communicate, consume news and enjoy entertainment. The online social world is becoming more a part of our day-to-day lives and allows us to keep up with how individuals are living their lives, rather than only relying on mass communication media like TV and radio to get a glimpse of what's going on in the world.

That leads us to the good news – what's old is new again. Since the beginning of time, relationships have been at the forefront of everything we do. Building relationships isn't done through Facebook Ads or brand campaigns exclusively; they're formed individually one by one. Social media gives you the power to identify consumers who are speaking about your brand and your competition as well as the ability to engage them directly.

But these relationships need to be carefully fostered. Importantly, the relationship that you form with your customer needs to be a two-way dialogue, otherwise you're pushing out content for the sake of creating noise.

There are a few things to keep in mind for engaging digitally connected customers. Here's the formula:

Know your audience – who are they and what channels are they on?

If you're trying to engage younger consumers, you're more likely to find them on Instagram, Snapchat, Twitch and TikTok. Whereas if you're trying to sell to a working-class Millennial or older it's most likely going to be on Facebook where you can reach them. You should spend your time on the platforms where your customers live.

What value do you bring to your intended audience?

Do you have a product or service that solves a problem? If so, find people who are openly speaking about that problem and hook them directly. As a consumer, if I complain about a company and their competitor immediately swoops in to help me, I am more likely to take my business to that company or brand. Every company and product or service has a target customer who has needs; your job is to connect those needs by listening and engaging directly.

Who are your references?

If you own an apparel brand and are selling t-shirts on Shopify, who is buying them? Seriously ask yourself: who are these people and do they have any influence whatsoever digitally? Going forward, start keeping track of your customers digitally to see who they're connected to and form a dialogue with them in an attempt to leverage their influence within their circles. If someone buys from you and has a good experience, they're immediately a reference.

Who has perceived influence among your target consumers and how can you align with them?

For example, when younger consumers think of 'Yeezys' they aren't proudly representing Adidas but rather Kanye West. Who are the influencers that exist right now within your industry? These don't have to be international celebrities but can instead be thought leaders in your industry or local figures who have important influence within their communities. Whoever they are, you should be finding ways every day to form relationships with them; social media provides you with the opportunity to directly connect with and catch the attention of these individuals, rather than having to connect via a third party such as an agent.

Speaking of Kanye West and influencers, pay close attention to how the music industry is benefiting from the shift of brands being corporations to people being brands. Songs go viral too. Today, whenever a new album drops, people are taking to Instagram and Snapchat to share a screenshot of a hot new song playing on their iPhone from iTunes or Spotify. For the launch of West's album titled *Ye*, a private listening party was held in Wyoming, which included several notable influencers. The exclusive experience was one that could only be accessed digitally through social media, and it made the album an overnight success. Again, movements and experiences are what people crave to be a part of – something bigger than themselves.

Create your own influence

The power of influencers extends beyond the music industry into all sorts of other businesses, and brands have a prime opportunity not only to connect with the largest influencers but also harness the power of smaller influencers, such as employees and customers. Everyone has influence within their own circles, and tapping into these networks can help grow your reach exponentially.

Yet consider the travel industry, where a quick YouTube search for 'Best places to vacation' doesn't reveal a single video from Marriott, Hilton, Expedia or even an airline, but rather videos with millions of views from creators – who are hired by brands – to show consumers how a trip to a place like Bora Bora will change their lives, improve their marriage or make them happier. This kind of escape from reality is the dream that influencers are selling to the masses. Every brand can do this, and they should. In fact, having an employee or customer share their best vacation stories could be even more relatable and therefore powerful.

These examples are real-life instances that demonstrate the point I introduced earlier in the chapter: that today's brands aren't billion-dollar corporations, but everyday people steering other people down the path of purchase. The beauty of social media is that it gives power to all. However, what an entity does with that power is another story.

In 2016, Donald Trump became the President of the United States of America. In the lead-up to the election, his social media presence included a heavy dose of Facebook Ads. With a massive campaign budget, Trump was able to ensure that more people were mentioning his name – good or bad – than his adversary Hillary Clinton, in addition to seeing his campaign content.

This was a demonstration of the power of social media at its finest. Meaning, with the right mix of charisma, a large following, and content that's amplified by those loyal followers and ad budget, anyone in the future might have the formula to enhance their campaign for political office with social media. Pretty scary, huh?

What's even more eye-opening than Trump's social media assisted election victory is that the world's largest brands based on revenue are less influential (digitally) than the likes of hip-hop star DJ Khaled, Kim Kardashian West, Kylie Jenner and... an egg.

In 2019, an unknown group of social media influencers banded together to create a social experiment on how quickly you can manipulate human behavior. An Instagram account labelled 'World_Record_Egg' set out to see if they could get the most engagement on an Instagram post, ever – a world record previously held by Kylie Jenner. It worked. Not only did the post gain over 50 million 'likes' but the account itself received over 9 million followers. So yes, you could extrapolate this to conclude that a dull, brandless egg today is more engageable than your average consumer packaged goods (CPG) or consumer brand.

To that point, the most followed Instagram accounts as of April 2019, outside of Instagram itself, were owned by Cristiano Ronaldo (163 million), Ariana Grande (152 million), Selena Gomez (149 million), The Rock (140 million), Kim Kardashian West (136 million), Kylie Jenner (133 million), Beyoncé (127 million), Taylor Swift (116 million) and Lionel Messi (115 million) (Trackalytics, 2019). The only brands that even come close in follower size on Instagram are National Geographic (108 million) and Nike (87 million). On Facebook, some brands have built up similar-sized followings, such as Samsung (159 million) and Coca-Cola (107 million), yet these two brands only have a combined total of 6 million Instagram followers. It's safe to say that people gravitate to platforms like Instagram to follow celebrities, influencers and their friends.

So, is brand marketing a lost cause on social media? Not at all. Many companies have still found success, and the majority of consumers have made a purchase through a social media channel (Avionos, 2018).

It's no secret that social media offers a competitive advantage to corporate brands who are willing to invest time, money and people in building a community. However, if companies want to thrive in this new era, they must change their approach and be less a brand

and more human. Social media is just a tool – it's not the strategy, and it's not perfect.

Still, social media marketing can be challenging, and as such, many marketers try to justify their lack of success. The following common phrases, uttered around workplaces everywhere, are just some of the challenges the modern marketer faces every day:

> 'The platforms are constantly evolving.'
>
> 'Nobody knows how the algorithms work.'
>
> 'What worked last year doesn't work this year.'
>
> 'I have thousands of followers but low engagement.'
>
> 'It's not free.'

Struggling with these challenges is understandable – it's tricky new territory to be navigated. Social networks are a big business whereby we, the consumers, are trying to transact on rented land. Think of Facebook like you would a casino – nobody knows the house rules better than the house. Nobody can beat the house at its own game. However, like poker, you can play by the house rules and still come out victorious over those who aren't as skilled or knowledgeable about how the game is played.

It took me the better part of a couple of years in the early 2000s to figure out that building a personal brand was an asset that could lead me to gain press and notoriety for my then start-up. With an own brand came connections and awareness, through connections came cash and opportunities.

If you're still reading, there's a high likelihood that you are using social media in your business already. I applaud you. But I also implore you to consider carefully exactly *what* you are doing with it.

With the rise of social media, digital advertising, brand building and social media influencers, the business of growing businesses is not linear. There may be stops and starts along the way, and the role of a marketer is far from easy, but it helps when you know the formula and the systems. Where do your customers go to consume information? Go there with them. Be a part of their life. Speak to them in the manner that they are being spoken to by their friends. Chances are their Facebook buddy isn't saying 'Hey Steve, want to know what the secret is to losing weight? Click on the link below to download my 5-step program!'

Just as consumers have become accustomed to flipping the channel any time a commercial airs, we now swipe or scroll past a brand that we perceive to be advertising to us. As such, it's more important than ever to speak like a human rather than a brand that's selling something.

The most effective marketers that I have encountered personally over the last several years are entrepreneurs who follow me across various platforms: they know what I do for fun, they know what my habits and hobbies are, and they wait for that right moment – for me to say something along the lines of… 'Need to lose a few pounds, any recommendations?' – before they slide into my DMs to offer me a free 15-minute coaching call before upselling me to join their virtual fitness boot camp. That's not sales. That's not marketing. That's being present in someone's life. And guess what? It isn't something that you can automate.

Most brand marketers that I meet want to have the biggest Instagram account in their industry. They think that if they don't have a Facebook page with millions of 'likes' they're not hitting critical mass, but they're wrong. You don't need thousands or millions to succeed in this game. But you do need people who care enough about your company to tell their friends about you. It's no different from network marketing or multi-level marketing.

Several months ago, I had a conversation with a chief marketing officer (CMO) who told me that she was looking for an agency who could help her brand engage with their 30 million Facebook page followers. My immediate answer to her wasn't in the form of a plan to engage 30 million followers because I know for a fact that would be impossible. Instead, it was to educate her on why engagement is low, in several points:

- Facebook reach is 1 per cent or less organically – that's 29.7 million people gone.

- Even then, these remaining 300,000 people, on average, are not 'seeing' the brand's content much less engaging with it because the brand is always in hyper-sales mode.

- As a brand, they would have to spend massive amounts of cash to reclaim the desired reach she was seeking.

I suggested that she should utilize my company, to focus on engaging 0.1 per cent of their total community to identify who is of influence and who cares about the brand.

To be candid, my agency didn't land the account, probably because I was too blunt and didn't over-promise on something that I know isn't realistic, whereas another agency may have offered that CMO the answer she was looking for.

The 0.1 per cent represents an audience of 30,000 Facebook users, which of course is far smaller than their 30 million followers and even the 300,000 who might organically see their posts. But even with that smaller group, only about 1 per cent can realistically be expected to not just see the content but actively engage with it. That's 300 people **not** 30 million.

Now, we are talking about a micro-fraction of a brand's audience – which is laughable to most executives – but let me break this down for you even further. If I were to put 300 people in a room right now, you wouldn't be able to speak to 300 people in an hour and carry meaningful dialogue. It's just not possible. It's a lot of people in 'real life'.

Let's say out of those 300 Facebook users who care about this brand you are now able to form a relationship with 10 per cent of them, that's 30 people who are your 'super fans'. We just went from your company having 30 million worthless Facebook page followers to 30 people in this world who personify your brand each day. If I went to any CMO and brought them 30 advocates,

I don't know of a single one that would say 'no'. But this is a weird space that we're in.

Every decade there is a change of the guard in technology, there is a new medium by which we grow and scale and monetize and reach masses. To profit and benefit you need to be aware of where the current is headed.

For every person who is upset because Facebook is making it harder to reach critical mass, go back and re-read the formula that I just broke down for you. The only numbers game that is in play here is who is a qualified follower versus another random vanity metric. I like it when my colleagues doubt the power of social media because they aren't getting the engagement that they want on social media. It means there's more market share waiting to be consumed by those who do get it.

If I, a high-school dropout who didn't go to college to get an MBA in marketing, can figure out how to make sense of social media to grow a start-up before social media was 'a thing' for most businesses, so can you. It's not hard, and it's not rocket science, but there is a science behind it, which is what I'm here to teach you. Everything is easy if you understand the systems and where the current is headed.

While there are plenty of business books and resources that will teach you the basic principles of internet marketing and personal brand building, I'm not here to repeat what's already been said; I'm here to give you the guide that's going to keep you in business or a job.

The purpose of this book isn't to make you a better marketer but rather to make you a better businessperson and teach you how to leap your competition by building relationships at scale while using technology as your rocket ship.

It's all about embracing new school tools with old school rules. Historically, relationships were formed over drinks and golf. Today, Facebook is the hotel lobby bar and Twitter is the golf course. Marketing, as we know it, is dead.

The only choice you have is to evolve or die and if you choose to change, then you must learn the playbook that's actively being used by every successful influencer and agency around. Until then you are just swimming in a giant digital ocean hoping to find your way.

References

Avionos (2018) Avionos releases new data revealing how consumer expectations are driving retail strategies, 23 April [Online] https://www.avionos.com/avionos-releases-new-data-revealing-how-consumer-expectations-are-driving-retail-strategies/ (archived at https://perma.cc/ZTR5-CCMP) [accessed 24 April 2019]

Internet World Stats (2019) World internet users and 2019 population stats, March 2019 [Online] https://www.internetworldstats.com/stats.htm (archived at https://perma.cc/X6Y5-EYYU) [accessed 24 April 2019]

The Fortnite Team (2018) Announcing 2018–2019 Fortnite competitive season, Epic Games, 12 June [Online] https://www.epicgames.com/fortnite/en-US/news/announcing-2018-2019-fortnite-competitive-season (archived at https://perma.cc/RRT5-LJ6R) [accessed 24 April 2019]

Trackalytics (2019) The most followed Instagram profiles, 24 April [Online] https://www.trackalytics.com/the-most-followed-instagram-profiles/page/1/ (archived at https://perma.cc/93J8-6FTD) [accessed 24 April 2019]

02
Stranded in a digital ocean

The internet is a noisy place, and it's only going to get louder as companies like Facebook and Google gain more control over how we consume digital content and communicate.

With the rise of streaming services such as Hulu and Netflix and online shopping via Amazon, we are quickly becoming dependent on smart technology that forces us – consumers – to be online all the time. We are no longer in the internet era of the 1990s and early 2000s where you could sign off and go about your everyday life. With the rise of these services alongside social media, smart technology is your life. And the world – even the most remote parts of it – is becoming more connected every day.

And these companies are increasingly playing a direct role in facilitating this connection. For example, during Facebook's annual F8 conference in 2018 I sat in the audience, amazed to learn about the company's plans to bring Wi-Fi to more communities around the world. At the time of writing, Facebook has partnered with internet service providers and mobile network operators to bring its Express Wi-Fi product to eight countries, such as India, Indonesia and Kenya (Express Wi-Fi by Facebook, 2019). If Facebook can operate like the utility company that provides me with an internet connection in my home, can they replace cable television through Facebook Watch? Can they replace my cellular phone provider, too, if my iPhone has a permanent internet connection allowing me to use WhatsApp or Messenger for phone calls and text messaging? More importantly, can they have unlimited,

24/7 access to what I am talking about to others and searching online, and use this data to serve me custom ads?

The answer is yes – they could, and to an extent they already are.

At the same Facebook F8 conference, I experienced virtual reality (VR) social media for the first time through Facebook's Oculus technology. I was fully immersed in an environment where I was able to interact with other users, go on Facebook Live and even take a selfie while disguised as a cartoonish avatar. Imagine when the world that we live in today allows you to go online not as yourself, but rather as an avatar, which you design to your own liking.

The lines between reality and virtual reality are becoming increasingly blurred. Eventually, Mark Zuckerberg will fulfil his objective of 'bringing the world closer together' (Zuckerberg, 2017), which in many aspects he already has. To put the numbers into perspective, there are 7.72 billion people on the planet as of March 2019 (Internet World Stats, 2019). And as of 31 March 2019 there are 2.38 billion monthly active users on Facebook (Facebook, 2019).

But, what if there's more to Facebook potential for world domination that neither you nor I can see yet? I'm not a conspiracy theorist by any means, but I do look at life through an objective lens and always feel that there's more than what meets the eye. Many marketers and people who use social media in their business fall into the trap of only thinking about right now.

You might currently be asking yourself:

- How am I going to meet my sales numbers?
- How am I going to obtain KPIs?
- How am I going to get more engagement?

These short-term questions are obviously important and understandable for anyone who's trying to grow their business. But there is also a single, long-lens question that you need to continually ask yourself: How am I going to stay relevant?

The answer lies in part in harnessing what makes your brand unique. In the digital ocean of social media, you need a way to stand out, because there are so many brands as well as individuals on social media today contributing to the overload of content. While you might see some 17-year-old kids who have more clout than the Ferraris they rent, or make-up artists on YouTube that have more fandom than MAC Cosmetics, standing out on social media is not easy by any means – especially for a brand. We are all competing against each other for consumers' limited amount of time and attention.

Adding to the challenge of standing out is the difficulty of standing the test of time. Very few posts have long shelf lives; instead, the lifespan of content on social media can range anywhere from a few seconds to a few minutes on average. And if you don't immediately get engagement on your posts, it's as good as you never posting at all. However, there are ways to improve shelf life by posting and engaging more like a person than a brand. To better understand this concept, try doing this as a 'test'. Look up two or three of your favorite brands on Instagram and analyze the following:

- When was the last time that they posted?
- How far apart are their three most recent posts?
- When was the last comment?

Now, go to Facebook and see how long it takes for you to see any brand in your newsfeed with a non-sponsored, 'organic' post. See when that post was created and compare it against the first ten posts in your newsfeed. Do the same for Twitter while you're at it.

In conducting this test, there's a good chance you'll find sporadic organic posting from brands, compared with the frequency at which individuals post and engage. People are checking on their social media accounts throughout the day, posting often, and coming back multiple times a day to follow up and converse. They are the ones who are carrying the conversation on social media, while brands, in many cases, are not truly socializing. Many brands only post once every few days, and when they do, they're often trying to get you to buy something from them. Even if they are posting daily, it often looks as if they are posting merely because they feel that they have to, such as tweeting out a link to a product page, and as a result the brand gets little to no engagement.

If you are a personal brand or represent a corporate brand and are becoming increasingly frustrated because whenever you post it seems as if nobody is paying attention, the reality is you don't have a social media presence. Instead you are on social media making noise, and sadly nobody is paying attention. Don't feel bad; you are not alone in this challenge. As an entrepreneur or business owner, social media can be mentally draining, and as a corporate marketer it's not any easier. It's a lot of maintenance and more complex than people assume.

The fact is: you can't post content – no matter how good it is – and walk away.

On the contrary, if your content resonates and appeals to a specific audience, these people will 'like, comment and share', and this is when you need to dive in further. You must be prepared to engage within your posts, such as by commenting on other people's comments.

Remember how I said before that the life expectancy of a post ranges anywhere from a few seconds to a few minutes? The next time you're on any social network refresh your newsfeed and see how fast the content displayed changes. Your feed could look completely different within just a few seconds. But post engagement is how you combat this. For every occasion where there's an engagement action on that post, it gives your post a 'bump' within the algorithm, giving it added priority in newsfeeds and extending the life expectancy ever so slightly.

Getting social media users to engage

It's clear you want people to engage. Now, how do you get them to engage?

First, from my experience, any time that I publish a post that is thought-provoking it tends to get people talking or commenting. Questions tend to be particularly useful for getting your audience to actually respond rather than just thinking about the post. For example, you can ask questions like:

- What's your favorite social network?
- Who do you recommend as a graphic designer?
- What's the best investment you made in the last year?
- What type of content would you like to see me create?
- What's a brand that's over-delivering on social media?
- How may I help you?
- What's your favorite emoji?

These are all very basic, entry-level posts that are text-based, which I've used throughout the years to gain what I refer to as 'cheap engagement', but it's engagement nonetheless.

The other tactic is what I refer to as 'value-tainment' otherwise known as giving your target audience 'Did you know?' facts, figures or tips to help them become better at marketing or whatever activities your audience engages in. It's also not uncommon for me to read an article in *TechCrunch* related to social media and then take to my 'Social Media Masterminds Group' on Facebook or head over to Twitter and share my thoughts as a way of giving insights to my followers. Brands can similarly comment on trending news stories or share fun facts, such as a software company posting productivity hacks or commenting on work–life balance debates. These are all forms of 'value add' or value-tainment.

The point is, if any of these social networks detect that people are engaging with your content, you are automatically perceived to have some influence. Whether that's true or not is less relevant; it's an algorithm that you're going up against.

Let's break down the strategy of these posts. I work in social media marketing, and I own a marketing agency. Therefore, it's in my best interest to start conversations with people in my industry who share similar interests. In some cases, I use short, text-based, thought-provoking posts as lead generation or to gather ideas for content which I can, later on, monetize through ads or course sales. This is the purpose of social media – it's socializing first and foremost.

What I will then do shortly after sharing one of my smart 'engagement bomb' posts is follow up with a new video or photo-based post that's intended to drive an end user to my website or a third-party website such as YouTube. (To be clear, this tactic of giving upfront value through info-sharing or conversation starting primarily works on Twitter, LinkedIn and Facebook. On a platform such as Instagram you're forced to lead in with an eye-catching photo or video. However, the same principles apply to posting a question in your caption to get people commenting.)

Regardless of what industry you work in, if you want to grow a following, you should be taking to social media to speak more about the space you're in and the products or services you sell – again, you should be socializing. That means not just sending out content in the hope it reaches someone, but taking a targeted approach and starting conversations with specific people, eg, via the direct message (DM) feature available on many social platforms.

For example, since joining Twitter in April 2009, I can't tell you how many times I've tweeted and immediately shared that tweet with 50 to 100 of my closest followers privately via DM to get an organic bump in engagement within the first few minutes of pushing out a tweet. The same goes for Instagram, where I've created various 'share groups' to get my content in front of users within seconds of a post going live on my page in the hope they will like and comment within the post.

These tactics might seem over the top or take you out of your comfort zone, but it's all part of the game of standing out in a noisy digital ocean. You either sink or swim.

This strategy has always been a secret of how I run my social media presence. To be candid, everyone who's someone online is breaking through the digital noise using a combination of Facebook Ads, engagement pods, buying likes, auto-engagement bots and virtual assistants. However, one fact remains clear – content is queen and community is king, and they need to work together to create an empire. If you aspire to stand out in the crowded and noisy digital ocean that is social media, you can't just sit idle; you must have genuinely good content, self-promote, and then slowly build a tribe of followers who will promote for you.

The reason why many people and brands fail fast on social media is because despite doing 'all of the right things' (ie, posting daily across multiple social networks, creating visually pleasing content, etc), nobody's paying attention to them, or if some are, they aren't being engaged in a meaningful dialogue or relationship by the brand.

We are all the digital equivalent of Tom Hanks in the movie *Castaway* sending SOS signals for 'help!' I often refer to this analogy in my keynote presentations. In the movie, Hanks's character spends the majority of the film developing ways to get off a deserted island while trying to stay alive. In the film, he creates an imaginary character out of a volleyball, which he names 'Wilson'. Throughout the story, Hanks's character tries his hardest to get off the island but to no avail until the very end. In our worlds as marketers, whenever you tweet or post and get little to no engagement, you're speaking to your version of 'Wilson' the volleyball – yourself. Your digital SOS signal on social media stands for 'same old stuff' in the hope that someone sees your content and takes action. So, let's change that.

Be where your customers are

Getting others to receive your signal starts with having a presence where 'they' – your customers – are. Don't be everywhere for the sake of trying to reach everyone because you can't possibly be on every social network and be above average. The likelihood is that you work in an industry or offer a solution or service that appeals to a specific demographic, therefore you should only be on the one or two social networks where your target audience has the most significant presence.

By placing yourself on the social networks where your target demographic spends their time, and removing yourself from the others which don't make sense for your business, not only will you have more time to dive deeper into certain social networks but you will also immediately be competing with fewer people for digital eyeballs.

For example, if your business is B2B, you don't necessarily need to be on Instagram, Snapchat or Twitter whereas LinkedIn and Facebook are a must-have. Depending on your business, you might be able to go 'all in' on LinkedIn only and resort to Facebook for just ad placement.

The flipside of this argument, however, is centered around using your employees to broaden your reach. Your business overall can benefit from multiple social networks if your employees engage on these platforms as representatives of your brand in some way. For example, assume that you're in a B2B organization with 50 sales representatives. I would highly recommend that you stick to one corporate social network, making that your go-to platform to spotlight customer stories and other relevant insights that your target customer would find valuable first. Then, have your employees hit social media hard across Twitter, Instagram, Facebook and LinkedIn as the faces of your brand, versus trying to create corporate channels everywhere and come across as mediocre.

There's more to come on the topic of employee advocacy in Chapter 8. However, you need to start thinking about activating an army of employees singing your company's praises across a wide network, so that even if you only focus on one corporate channel, you can still reach customers where they are. I look at standing out on social media as an orchestra. I'm one person, and you are one person; alone our voices and instruments can only go so far and might not sound all that amazing. But together, we can amplify our voices and create a symphony of sound. Imagine that concept multiplied by dozens, hundreds or thousands of employees who can help spread your message across their networks.

Gaining this reach takes time, but unfortunately, I've worked for and with many brands that only focus on achieving an instant return on investment (ROI). If that's what you're looking for, you're in the wrong business. Instead, the focus should be on creating long-lasting relationships digitally with customers. Likewise, if you don't like people you're definitely in the wrong place.

That's not to say that it's easy to focus on the long term. In the past, I've been guilty of falling into the trap of looking for instant results instead of genuine, interested engagement. Many times in previous corporate roles my team and I would spend months coming up with social media communication plans for key stakeholders, which would outline to a T what we were going to post or share across the various social networks. We'd have this grandiose plan, which would begin with an initial post on campaign launch day, followed by more posts throughout a specific time frame, followed by measuring the results and reporting up the chain of command to our leaders. To be truthful, I always found ways to spotlight the good but never the bad – and it's an easy fallback I still see many social media managers make. Enthusiastically, I'd report to our chief marketing officer (CMO) the millions of impressions that we generated and thousands of engagements – many of which were gamed or automated by bots that would 'engage' with a post which contained specific hashtags. A lot of it was 'fluff' to mask the obvious: nobody cared and nobody was paying attention.

But like anything else in life, you learn over time how to optimize and improve. If there's one thing that working in social media for over a decade has taught me, it is that we are operating at the mercy of the social networks themselves. And this means brands need to constantly adapt.

For example, I firmly believe that if Facebook wants you to succeed, they will make you successful. Now, how do they measure you versus me versus the next person? It's in time spent. If you're driving people to YouTube and keeping them around – even if they click away from your channel – you're helping Google serve up more ads; therefore, you are an influencer in the form of a referral source to them. Have you ever wondered why Influencer A on

YouTube doesn't have as active a presence or as big a following on Facebook? Meanwhile, Influencer B has a million followers on Instagram, yet they have a smaller audience on YouTube. It's in Google's best interest to build up 'stars' on their platform (YouTube) than to allow them to venture off to Facebook. And vice versa, the same rules apply to Facebook.

Likewise, focusing only on driving people off these networks and to your site could backfire. The networks themselves are not designed to make your job easy, and they aren't in place for you to grow your business for free either. In addition to competing against other people and brands, you're fighting against an algorithm that's designed to detect sales rhetoric and spam from brands and advertisers (as well as people) who are trying to grow their business at the expense of Facebook or whatever network you're using.

If you want to know how to game the algorithm, you need to be unique and create genuine engagement rather than directly asking people to 'like, comment, share', because Facebook wants you to pay for that. The next time that you head over to your Facebook Ads manager, take a look at the objectives underneath – 'What's your marketing objective?' – and pay attention to each one of them. Whether it's driving website clicks, increasing engagement on your most recent post, or driving views to a recently uploaded video, Facebook is expecting you to pay for results

If you continue to use social media as if it's still 2010 your brand will die. You must strive to be different even if that means you're sliding into hundreds of DMs per day to get your audience's attention. As I said at the beginning of the chapter, just creating content for the sake of having something to say isn't going to cut it.

Analyze what content works

Through my business now, Gil Media Co, I have the opportunity to work with a variety of corporate clients and advise them on what they should be doing. Whenever I'm working with a client, I spend a significant amount of time analysing the content that their competition is pushing out, as well as metrics that are publicly available.

You can run these searches for free within Facebook, Instagram, Twitter, etc, to see what your competitors are doing and how their performance compares with your own. If you want to dive deeper, affordable software like Sprout Social (which I often use) makes it easy to publish content, see how it performs and run an analysis on competitors. The least of my concerns is the number of followers that the brand has, because I know very well there's a likelihood that back in the early 2010s someone on my client's social media team, as well as the social media teams at their competitor brands, were focused on acquiring followers. In reality, those followers are inactive and not paying attention to what's being posted.

When conducting this initial analysis, I look closely at the following:

- Number of engagements during a period to see if there's a particular day or time where the client's community is more active so we can ensure they're consistently hitting the newsfeed during peak times.

- The type of content that's seeing the most significant spikes in engagement so we can work with our client on creating more of the same (ie, photos versus videos).

- How posting frequency affects engagement – if the brand doesn't post daily, this usually results in a drastic decline in engagement.

- Which posts over the last quarter performed the best – these are the posts that should be circled back to, in order to reply to comments from users that were missed, re-share the post or tweet a slight variation to bring it back into the newsfeed. It's also important to try to identify why these posts performed better than others.

- Who explicitly is engaging consistently – specifically, what do we know about our community and are we engaging them directly?

After analysing the activity from the client themselves, I then look at the competition to see what I can uncover and take away as best practice and opportunities for my client.

For example, if Competitor A is mainly posting short, less than 30-second videos on Facebook, which are getting high view counts and engagement made possible by Facebook Ads, then I recommend to my client that they follow the same approach but with video content that's more visually appealing. If Competitor B sees low engagement on Instagram because they're drowning out their community with stock photography, then I encourage my client to scrap stock photos altogether and use lifestyle photos of employees or customers. If Competitor C posts every other day but on the days in-between posting they're ensuring that their community management team is interacting with their community, I recommend to my client that they (the client) publish daily as well as engaging within the overall population of buyers to 'one-up' Competitor C.

The power of leveraging competitive insights is priceless. Indeed, 'the devil is in the detail' of the data that you can present to your boss or client.

When you analyze what the field is doing, you instantly have insight into what's working and what's not. The beauty of competition on social media is that you're competing for the attention of the same demographic on a level playing field. Just because other brands in your industry are more well-known than yours doesn't suddenly give them access to an exclusive tool or feature that you don't have access to.

For example, McDonald's, Burger King and Wendy's all sell cheeseburgers but what makes you follow each of them on social media – and buy from them – is predicated on what they post, where they post and when they post it. Your content, like these brands, should be so damn good that people will want to share it with their friends. That's the key to success. McDonald's, Burger King and Wendy's are all speaking to the same audience of people who love to eat cheeseburgers. And they're all saying essentially the same thing, but it's the brand which is perceived to be the most personable and fun-to-follow that wins the digital market share.

For example, there are so many software brands competing for market share, but ones like Adobe stand out on social because they create content their audience can relate to. Rather than just posting about new features for their different software products, for instance, Adobe shares content such as beautiful wildlife photography on Instagram to engage its user base of photographers, or creating native videos on Facebook interviewing leaders in technology to talk about AI to engage its more technical user base.

TOP TIP

Speaking of market share, beware of 'digital pirates' who are out to steal your followers away from you. Whether it's through ad targeting or ruthless community management, which I refer to as 'savagery', the most skilled marketers today have access to poach your followers – easily. For example, they can respond directly to customers who comment on your posts, they can view your list of followers and reach out to them, and they can search for the customers who are mentioning your brand but not receiving engagement from you, which provides an opportunity for your competitor to step in.

You should never lose sight of the word 'social' in social media if you hope to stand out and thrive. Ask yourself: are you socializing or are you solely trying to sell? Every day, I get messages from people who are hustling me and other users to buy Bitcoin, or fake 'followers' to appear credible. In these times you need to hunker down in the community that you're building because it's the power of community that will help your brand stay above water while everyone else drowns trying to figure it out.

Less promotion, more interaction

If you're old enough to remember those Billy Mays commercials for 'As Seen on TV' products in the US, then you'll understand where I'm going with this: social media is the new infomercial.

Everywhere you turn you're being sold a dream or an illusion of wealth, whether it's going on Facebook to see a marketer advertise his overpriced 'exclusive' masterclass or Tai Lopez teaching you the steps to growing infinite wealth. That's not content, it's noise.

Brands are so desperate to sell that they're killing off any momentum they built up in the days before social media became pay-to-play. Think about your own experience when using social media. If you don't enthusiastically enjoy seeing brand content in your feed, you are confirming this notion.

I understand sales are an important metric for any business. But I also know that if I used social media as a platform to continually promote myself or my business, nobody would care or pay attention. Instead, I've been able to successfully transition from working as a corporate marketer to creating my own marketing agency due to building relationships on social media over the past decade and creating content that demonstrates that I'm an authority in my field. So, if the reason you're on social media is to drive more revenue for your business – join the club. We're all here for the same reason but how you get there will vary from the next person.

Whether you're a personal brand trying to get brand deals or a corporate brand trying to outshine your competition, you *must* adhere to the principles of digital marketing etiquette, the first and most important of which is 'less promotion and more interaction'. Always keep in mind that 'clicks', 'reach', 'impressions', etc, are just numbers, but behind those numbers is a person. Who are they? Make it your goal moving forward to go deep down the funnel of getting to know who your customers are. If you want to build an army of advocates, it begins with first getting a handful of customers, fans and followers to have a direct dialogue with you.

Every one of these social networks gives you reach and access to make this possible. There's not one social network that is better than any other in my opinion. As I mentioned earlier, my recommendation always has been, and still will be, to go where your audience is. This is why whenever I'm asked: 'Should I be on Instagram instead of Snapchat?' I always turn it around and ask 'Where's your audience?'

Once you've found and established your audience, you can then think about sales. Sales are one to one. They always have been and will continue to be. The biggest mistake marketers make is thinking they're going to get on social media and immediately have reach and make sales to an abundance of people. The reality is that people have tuned out brands the same way they've tuned out commercials on the television or the radio, so you need to focus less on getting big numbers quickly and focus more on building small relationships that eventually add up.

Knowing that content is irrelevant within minutes of posting, you should also be prioritizing conversations, whether that's in your comments, DMs or if it moves offline. A conversation is very different from a single tweet or a well-produced video that is only seen once; it can carry on indefinitely, and most importantly, it gets to the heart of why many people are on social media in the first place – to be heard and to connect with others.

So how can you harness this for your brand's benefit? Acknowledge those who are engaging with you. 'Like' other people's content. Human emotion can't be measured like a traditional KPI, but it's a dominant currency. Making a person feel wanted is the difference between having thousands of followers who might never buy from you versus a person who's going to tell all of their friends about you and encourage them to buy from you.

People have the same amount of control and access as brands do to spread the word on social media, and you can leverage that fact to your advantage. Don't waste away the opportunity just because these conversations don't offer instant ROI. No potential customer gives a damn about your latest sale, but they do care about how you make them feel.

References

Express Wi-Fi by Facebook (2019) [Online] https://expresswifi.fb.com/ (archived at https://perma.cc/SQN4-EAKX) [accessed 24 April 2019]

Facebook (2019) Stats, 31 March [Online] https://newsroom.fb.com/ company-info/ (archived at https://perma.cc/S5K9-2ZMP) [accessed: 24 April 2019]

Internet World Stats (2019) World internet users and 2019 population stats, March 2019 [Online] https://www.internetworldstats.com/stats. htm (archived at https://perma.cc/X6Y5-EYYU) [accessed 24 April 2019]

Zuckerberg, M (2017) Bringing the world closer together [Blog] Facebook, 22 June [Online] https://www.facebook.com/notes/ mark-zuckerberg/bringing-the-world-closer-together/ 10154944663901634/ (archived at https://perma.cc/TQ6J-C9XP) [accessed 24 April 2019]

03

How to be savage AF – like Randy

Since early childhood, I have been an avid fan of pro wrestling. One of my earliest memories as a kid is from 1991, when as an 8-year-old I tuned into WWF *Superstars* one Saturday morning and watched in awe as Hulk Hogan was pummeled by The Undertaker and other 'bad guys', commonly referred to in wrestling terminology as 'heels'.

In those days Hulk Hogan was the 'good guy' that all of my elementary school friends cheered on. If YouTube had existed back then, Hulk would have been the Jake Paul of that era – a highly popular alpha male adored by a pre-teen audience. The reason why that moment stands out is that it was rare to see a 'face', which is the proper term for a hero-like figure such as Hulk Hogan, to get beaten up by a heel, or in this case a group of them.

As I grew up so did my obsession with pro wrestling, the WWF and WCW. Not only did I collect the action figures and video games, but I attended several live events that my parents took me to, which made me begin to analyze the world of scripted entertainment. Then, as an early teenager and before I was able to drive a car, my interests shifted from playing with action figures to fantasy wrestling and role playing, which originated during the days of America Online (AOL) and chat rooms.

What younger generations today (ie, Generation Z) don't understand is that in the early days the internet – in those times of AOL – operated almost identically to today's social networks. Starting with the adrenaline rush of hearing the 'Welcome!' on AOL, you would see how many emails were in your inbox (the first notifications), you could chat with strangers in chat rooms (the original Twitter) and you could have private conversations on Instant Messenger (the modern-day snaps or private direct messages (DMs)). Really, not much has changed – except the platforms.

Although it wasn't cool to admit it, and nobody that I went to middle school with at the time knew, from the age of 13 until around 16 I ran one of the most active wrestling role-playing leagues online, known as the 'Fantasy Wrestling Federation' or 'FWF'.

For those who are curious, the way fantasy wrestling worked is that you would either create a fictitious character or pick an already existing one from 'real life', ie, a pro wrestler, and as this character you would send mass emails to the entire league. In these emails, you would type out your dialogue as if you were doing an in-ring interview, as seen on TV. Your imagination and creativity were vital. Then, weekly, you would compete against another player in your league. The winner was based on the quality of their email promos, and determined by the league commissioner or owner. Throughout these years, I did everything from recruiting fellow pro-wrestling fanatics to my league (we had around 30 to 40 participants, with about half of them being committed and active) to writing weekly match results and monthly pay-per-view results, which were quite lengthy, as I'm sure you can imagine. Then, occasionally someone would drop out and send an 'I quit!' email out to the entire league. This would force me to play backstage politics through private instant messaging (IM), in an attempt to prevent others from leaving. If it sounds like a mess, that's because it was.

However, in hindsight, I attribute my passion for storytelling and writing to my enthusiasm for pro wrestling, and specifically role playing. Not only did it teach me how to write a script, but it forced me to think creatively. I apply these skills every day as a digital storyteller – and that is what I want to teach you throughout this chapter.

Fast-forward to today, the WWF is now the WWE, which stands for 'World Wrestling Entertainment'. Keyword: 'entertainment'. There are two primary reasons why people go online and on social media today: to be educated or entertained. Most brands are not instinctively entertaining.

I'll go on record and say that 99 per cent of corporate brands active online today are boring; hence they take a back seat to celebrities and personal brands. In addition to feeling stale and boring, they lack personality.

Now, I know what it's like to work for a billion-dollar corporation. You're always under intense scrutiny to stay within the sandbox of being 'on brand', but this is social media – it's intended to be fun and engaging.

Outside of having to 'digital speak' a certain way, most often directed by a PR team, which gives marketing strict orders to stay within a set of stodgy brand guidelines, is the fact that you're speaking to people as a logo and not as a fellow person.

In a world where people trust where they eat thanks to Yelp recommendations made from strangers, or they take to Facebook to be influenced on what type of TV or car to buy because they ask their friends, it's a no brainer. People buy from people, not brands.

When you walk into your favorite consumer electronics store to buy a new TV, there's a good chance you'll take time to speak to a person working there to ask them for their suggestions, because even if you've researched what to buy, that individual's ideas and professional opinion matter. When these salespeople engage with you, they take the time to understand how you plan to use the TV and that conversation can lead to a recommendation that you trust more than a banner in a store advertising the latest features of a new TV. This concept of trusting personal recommendations transfers to social media. People tend not to tweet to @BestBuy, for example, to ask for recommendations, yet they'll take to social media to ask their friends for their thoughts on what to buy.

As such, employees of Best Buy or any other consumer brand should try to replicate that in-store personability and expertise online, including giving individual employees a voice online and ditching the corporate tone. The majority of today's consumers aren't going on social media to purposely seek out brand content (ie, they don't want to be sold to), but it is possible to flip the script and maintain an active brand presence by focusing on being entertaining and/or educational.

I often compare pro wrestling to social media marketing because of the similarities between scripted entertainment and planning out a social media content calendar. What people will see will determine how they react and take action. Likewise, the 'heel' and 'face' characters of pro wrestling are today's equivalent of a highly popular internet personality or a public figure that people openly hate and speak out against. Meanwhile, the factions that pro wrestling had in the 1990s such as the New World Order are today's version of two or more digital influencers collaborating to maximize their broadcast reach.

Going back to the early 1990s when the then-WWF had larger-than-life fictional characters, the younger version of myself lost sight of the fact that what I was watching on television wasn't real, but rather actors portraying the characters. The same can be said about online brands in the early 2010s. As social media was new for marketing, consumers thought it was cool that they could send a message to their favorite brand and overlooked the fact that the brand had a team of human beings behind it. However, as time went on and the brands faced internal pressure to justify the ROI of social media marketing, they overtly began to abuse their following by selling. And that's when the cool factor began to wear off.

Today, the way my adult self knows that pro wrestling isn't 'real' is the same way that consumers are not oblivious to the fact that their favorite brand on social media is run by a person or a team of people. Consumers want to see these personalities shine through rather than hear corporate-speak.

In a digital world where just about everyone wants to be a guru, an influencer or a star, it might be more apt to think of social media as the digital equivalent to *The X Factor* or *Britain's Got Talent*. It's very much a talent show, and content needs to make an impact rather than just asking for attention. One of the reasons why everyday people are seeing success online in terms of reach and subsequently growing a niche following is because they're giving their audience of viewers what they want to look at, over and over, without right-hooking them with a sales pitch. It's an easy concept to absorb, but do you see a business brand doing it effectively? If so, tweet me who it is, to @CarlosGil83, because I don't.

As a consumer, I find myself almost every evening going to YouTube on my smart television to binge-watch videos from noncelebrities who keep me entertained. There are videos about everything, from defunct rides at Disneyland to abandoned shopping malls, which I genuinely find fascinating and spend my time watching. Then, I put my marketing hat on and ask why my favorite brands aren't putting out the same style of infotainment videos or 'how-to' tutorials like my favorite YouTube creators are? What they're creating instead, which I see whenever I actually decide to run a search for my favorite brands, is content that looks, feels and speaks to me like a commercial. That's why I often suggest to brand marketers that they take several steps back and analyze the state of content today before creating another Facebook post that's going to fizzle out the moment they post it.

While most companies, and the marketers that work for them, are creating 12–18-month strategic plans, social media changes at such a rapid pace that it gives everyday users a competitive advantage over billion-dollar corporations who are operating at a turtle's pace to keep up and stay relevant. Instead of over-analysing where it's all headed, you need to be nimble and execute right now if you want to stay in the game long enough to see next month.

I am not an advocate of chasing the 'shiny new object', but I am a proponent of going where your audience is and riding the momentum wave that a new platform offers. Whenever there's a new app, and people are curious, the first set of users on that platform will benefit from those eyeballs that come to check it out. Belarusian–American entrepreneur Gary Vaynerchuk refers to this as a 'land grab' (Vaynerchuk, nd) if you're early enough and able to be one of the first to the party.

At the same time, be aware of the fact that platforms change quickly, and one day you might not be active on Twitter or Facebook anymore. However, the tactics behind relationship building and content marketing that you've learned can still be applied elsewhere. For example, many creators who once grew their entire brands on Vine were left on the outside when Vine was acquired by Twitter and then shut down, but the video creation principles used for Vine – being succinct and entertaining – are still applicable today.

Tomorrow, Twitch and TikTok could decide to open up their platforms to businesses, and an 'older' audience might flood the market, as we saw happen on Snapchat once brands discovered they had a direct bridge to younger consumers. Likewise, companies like Spotify and Amazon could jump into the social media game and then what? You have to be willing to pivot away from what's not driving tangible results and go to where the people are. This is also why you need to build a loyal community of followers and own their data (eg, email or phone number).

Be likeable but be a savage

To help you understand how to build a niche following and grow your bottom line at the expense of your competition, I am going to refer to one of my favorite wrestlers of all time, the late 'Macho Man' Randy Savage and one of my favorite Tom Hanks movies *Captain Phillips*.

Despite most kids my age in the early 1990s being 'Hulkamaniacs' (fans of Hulk Hogan), I thought that his yellow and red wrestling tights were lame in the same manner that I find content marketing dull and stale today. Therefore, I wasn't a fan of the Hulkster. Instead, there was one wrestler who I admired more than any others, and that was Randy Savage.

From his classic 'Oh yeah!' tagline and his iconic 'Pomp and Circumstance' entrance music, which you hear at every high school or college graduation, to his gaudy wrestling attire complete with a larger-than-life cowboy hat, Randy Savage was an innovator for his time and the true definition of standing out from his peers. Throughout his career, Randy Savage also evolved his character several times to stay fresh and up to date. Savage was ruthless, and like many other wrestlers of that era he built up a cult-like following by not being a 'cookie cutter' persona.

There is no disputing the fact that to grow your online business people need to like you before they buy from you. Although content marketing is one piece of the equation the other is community management. Without a community, you are only speaking to yourself. With a community behind you, you are able to put control of your valuable content in the hands of individuals who are more likely to share your content with pride to their legions of friends and followers. Community management goes beyond replying to customer enquiries as they arise; it's about paying attention to what's being said in the broader digital community about your brand, your competition and your industry.

Let's assume that your company has a dozen people who enthusiastically engage with your content whenever you post. Those dozen fans probably influence a small number of people in their circles; however, it's more meaningful for those dozen users to shout you out to their network than if you try to penetrate the same audience with an ad or a post because once again, consumers instinctively do not like to be advertised to. Realistically speaking, unless you're posting content that is either educational or entertaining it's not being shared or seen organically.

Now, as your engaged audience shares your message with their own networks, let's assume that you're able to turn those dozen 'super fans' into two dozen followed by 200 followed by 2,000. What if I told you that you could grow your fandom further by taking fans away from your competition – would you do it? This next lesson is where being a digital savage is the difference between someone who wants to win and someone that's okay with being average.

Social media isn't just a giant digital ocean; it's also the wild, wild West where listening is your most significant competitive advantage.

Right now, I want you to do the following:

> Go to Twitter or Instagram and type in #YourIndustry (eg, #RealEstate, #Insurance, #Sportswear, etc). What do you see?

On both platforms, it's likely you're seeing content similar to what you post for your own brand. Now, dig a little deeper, and in-between corporate or personal brand posts, you're likely to see content about your industry posted by either happy or angry customers.

This next step is where the 'fun' – and savagery – begins. You have a conscious decision to make first: go to where the customers are – even if that means finding them on competitors' channels or where they're talking about customers – or sit back and hope that customers somehow find you. Odds are you'll have more success being proactive and going after competitors' customers.

If you're doing any Facebook Ads it's likely you are used to running ad campaigns that target a specific group of users who like a particular brand similar to yours or share certain interests. This is great, but it's only scratching the surface. To be a savage, you must not care whose feelings outside of your company you are hurting. The playing field is business, and it's also a popularity contest: let's not forget both points in play.

Finding your brand mentions

Using the Twitter and Instagram examples, I would urge you to spend time curating the following search feeds in a tool like Hootsuite or Sprout Social:

> @yourbrand mentions + 'your brand' mentions + #yourbrand
> mentions

All too often companies will only respond to @reply or @mentions where the brand's username is tagged, but they will overlook organic brand mentions. This is an absolute oversight on the brand's part. If someone is upset, they're highly likely to blast your brand by using your @username in a post to get your attention, whereas I could be speaking about your brand to a friend in passing and mention it without necessarily feeling the need to get your attention (as is the case with hashtag mentions of a brand). I previously worked with a client who had over 1 million hashtag brand mentions (ie, #brandname) on Instagram, which had never been interacted with or managed. This example is a classic miss for most brands. Many will be the first to admit that they are understaffed and don't have the resources to reply to everyone, but this should be a priority above lower-value activities like creating a post asking people to visit your website.

Finding your brand mentions alongside competitor brands

In addition to setting up a search for your own mentions, I would also encourage monitoring your brand mentions alongside competitor brand mentions.

> @yourbrand mentions + @yourcompetition mentions + 'your
> brand' mentions + 'your competition' mentions + #yourbrand
> mentions + #yourcompetition mentions

This creates a real-time digital race to who will engage that customer first when customers mention your brand alongside a competitor in the same post. If they are mentioning your competitor in a post, it's for a reason and most likely because you haven't solidified a relationship with them. For example, money transferring services Western Union, Zelle and Venmo are all direct competitors of each other and will often be mentioned together in various tweets:

> 'My nana just asked me to send $ via @WesternUnion I haven't even been to one. uh, nana there's this app called @venmo and also @Zelle' @Twitter User, 1:16 pm, 27 May 2018

> 'Apple Pay, western union, money gram, Zelle yo pick' @Twitter User, 8:07 pm 28 May 2018

Yet none of the brands acknowledged these customers. In both cases the person tweeting could have been swayed to do business with any of these service providers had any of them swooped in and engaged. Imagine how special you would feel as a customer if you mentioned three companies and one of them chimed in offering to help?

Finding your competition's mentions in specific contexts

In addition to the broad searches you've set up, you should also create alerts for when customers are specifically talking about how they feel about your competitors.

> @yourcompetition mentions + 'your competition' mentions + #yourcompetition mentions + keywords such as 'sucks', 'hate', 'upset', 'mad', 'never again', 'don't buy' and 'love'

Here's where it gets dicey and a tad sensitive for most marketers. You're already underwater and trying to stay afloat with your brand mentions, now you're being asked to monitor your direct competitors. But remember, social media is the wild, wild West. There is nothing that says you cannot engage those who are speaking about your competition. For this next example, I am going to look at US supermarket Winn-Dixie and their direct competitor Publix. As I learned first-hand while working for Winn-Dixie, in the grocery business people are passionate about their baked goods. A quick search on Twitter for 'Publix Winn-Dixie cake' pulls up dozens of tweets like the ones below where real people are speaking about the brands, despite not directly tagging either one of them.

> 'I've never been more disappointed in my mother than I am today when she picked to get the girls a Winn Dixie cake over a Publix cake' @Twitter User, 10:35 am 20 October 2018

> 'Lmao I'm late, y'all boycotting Publix?? Man listen, as much as I absolutely hate Wal-mart, Publix Cake and fresh fruit, I just can't on this one. I participate(d) in that nasty a** high priced Starbucks coffee but I just can't with this one. Lol Hit me up on the Winn-Dixie boycott' @Twitter User, 5:16 pm 26 May 2018

Neither brand opts to jump into these conversations – which once again is a missed opportunity for creating brand awareness, gaining or keeping a customer. In either of these scenarios, a simple acknowledgement can go a long way toward earning goodwill with that customer. Moreover, incentivizing someone who's either had a poor experience with your brand or is a fan of your competition by sending them a gift card to shop with you can make all the difference. Yet silence from the brand completely ignores this opportunity. Imagine what you can do if you are able to see every time someone mentions that they 'hate' your competition or they tweet out that they 'will never buy' from them again? If you aren't tapping into these scenarios (which happen all too often) then you're clearly missing out.

An example of a brand that isn't afraid to jump into conversations about competitors and embodies what it means to be a digital savage is Wendy's. In 2018 when International House of Pancakes commonly known as 'IHOP' decided to change their name to 'IHOB' for International House of Burgers, Wendy's publicly roasted the chain on Twitter and effectively hijacked what otherwise would have been a moment in time for the IHOP brand to celebrate with the spotlight solely on them.

'Can't wait to try a burger from the place that decided pancakes were too hard.' @Wendys, 11:26 am 11 June 2018

Using industry mentions to find prospective customers

'your industry' mentions + 'looking to buy ___', 'recommendations for ___'

In many cases people mention the goods, products or services that you offer even if they don't directly mention your brand name or a competitor. Tap into searches around industry chatter often in order to grow your industry influence and client base. Let's face it, everyone wants to be seen, heard and acknowledged otherwise they wouldn't be taking to social media to publicly post, so don't be shy about hopping into these conversations. Remember, people have the same amount of control and access as brands do, so search queries run both ways. The good news is it's highly unlikely that others in your space are following these steps at the moment – that is until they read this book.

Monitoring reviews of your brand

> Reviews left on your Facebook page + your competitor's
> Facebook page

When I worked at Winn-Dixie and Save-A-Lot, I lived for the thrill of a bad product review because it was an opportunity to publicly showcase how much my team and I valued the unsatisfied customer's business while further showing our commitment directly to the customer. Most brands hate negative sentiment shown toward their company and will often try to 'sweep it under the rug'. Many social media managers are reviewed annually by their bosses based on net promoter score (NPS). While negative customer experience isn't something that you have complete control of on the social media team, you can undoubtedly steer how a customer thinks about you going forward once you've had an opportunity to address their concern. The best way to handle a negative comment or tweet (example: 'Publix Winn-Dixie cake' search) is to address it head on, not ignoring that it exists. By using key phrases like 'Thank you' and 'We appreciate your business' you're able to quickly defuse a situation online, get a customer over to your support team through private and direct conversation, and also show public onlookers that you care. Try this: go to your competitors' Facebook pages and purposely look out for negative reviews. Are they replying or is there an open window of opportunity for you to swoop in and convert that user to a new customer?

Engaging with your competitors' social media ads

> Comments + likes on Facebook or Instagram Ads

I'm all about growth hacking the system and getting clever when it comes to customer acquisition. The very next time that you come across a social media ad for your competitors, take a look at who is engaging with their ad. Since they're already doing the heavy lifting by absorbing the cost of user targeting, it's likely that whoever is engaging with their ad content is someone that you would also pay to reach. Look at the profile of who's engaging and engage with them back. Rarely does a brand engage in the comments section of an ad, which opens up the door for you to walk right in.

Once again, spend more time listening to what is said about your brand, your competition and industry, and less time posting content if you truly want to build community. Social media networks can operate as a real-time source of leads and clients; however, you need to make the first move and insert yourself into the conversation – even when you're not invited to, as is the case with Wendy's.

In the last chapter, I referenced Tom Hanks's role in *Castaway*, where his character is stranded on a remote island far away from civilization, and compared today's social media posts to Hanks's SOS cries for help in the movie – hardly anyone's paying attention.

Besides *Castaway*, another Tom Hanks movie that's a favorite of mine is *Captain Phillips*, in which a group of pirates from Somalia take Hanks's character's boat hostage. In the famous takeover scene, the head pirate says to Hanks's character 'Look at me, I'm the captain now.' Every day your brand is taken hostage by digital pirates starting with the social networks themselves and ending with fellow brands and digital creators who are taking views and market share away from you. So instead of playing it safe and letting others take over your social media ship, you need to be the one leading the conversation.

Strategies to change how your company is perceived on social media

Here are proven strategies you can implement to change how your company is perceived on social media:

1 Have a personality like Wendy's. Be funny, witty, sarcastic and, most important, be personable (remember the keyword in 'social media' is 'social'). With the rise of Generation Z, today's digital consumer is getting younger, and thus youth culture should be reflected in your brand marketing if you are trying to appeal to this demographic. Despite not being the top or even second-largest fast-food hamburger chain in the world, the Wendy's hip, cool and fun personality makes you want to follow them to see what they're going to say next. As evidenced in the example earlier, Wendy's is not only taking jabs at IHOP, but they're also not afraid of taking digital blows at McDonald's. If you must, go to UrbanDictionary.com to educate yourself on what the kids are saying these days and find ways to insert slang and catchy sayings into your content – trust me on this one.

2 Be a troll to the trolls. The internet today is full of negative people whose sole objective is to get a reaction from others. These individuals are commonly referred to as 'trolls' or 'haters'. If you really want to show internet bullies who's the boss and make a statement that your brand has a voice and personality, troll back the next time a troll comes across your newsfeed. In the example below, Tesco Mobile replied to a troll poking fun at the brand and gained nearly 2,000 retweets from the humorous dialogue. It's a great example of how to show that your brand has a personality, is funny, and engaging.

'Worst thing about me mother not answering her phone, is her voicemail reminding me that she's on the absolute poverty Tesco Mobile' @Twitter User, 2 July 2016

'Nah the worst thing is your own mother blatantly ignoring your calls.' @tescomobile, 5:58 am 3 July 2016

3 Think of your content like 'digital candy' that your audience will want to come back for more of. An example of a brand that also speaks to younger consumers and has done an excellent job at staying relevant throughout the years is Taco Bell. Like Wendy's, Taco Bell has always been an innovator when it comes to showing us marketers how to effectively do social media.

In 2015, Taco Bell created a GIF generator whereby you'd tweet your favorite emoji + the taco emoji to @TacoBell, and they would tweet you back with a custom GIF. Speaking of GIFs and making your content appear to be lively, Twitter, Facebook and Instagram all have integration with Giphy, which is the Google of GIFs. You can leverage GIFs in your posts and replies to add emotion, or you can add an emoji or two as well. If you're trying to go outside of the social media box, create your own company-branded GIFs and upload them to Giphy. If selected, your GIFs will now be accessible to billions of users across social media. A quick search on Giphy.com for Taco Bell's account shows that their GIFs have generated over 1 billion lifetime views! How cool is that?

4 In addition to trolling your customers back, it's perfectly okay to troll your competition and troll yourself too. In 2017, Hostess Snacks tweeted out on the day of the solar eclipse only to be trolled by competitor MoonPie who didn't say much other than 'Lol ok', a phrase equivalent to brushing off something you perceive to be lame. The bigger story was the nearly 200,000 retweets and over 500,000+ likes that MoonPie was able to gain at the expense of Hostess Snacks.

The next example comes from McDonald's, which poked fun at itself in 2017 after posting 'Black Friday ***Need copy and link***'. After this apparently public mistake, they humorously followed up with a promotion for their coffee.

'When you tweet before your first cup of McCafé... Nothing comes before coffee.' @McDonaldsCorp, 6:48AM, 24 November 2017

5 When you have search queries set up for 'your brand' minus the @reply or @mention, you're able to get a better view of what's really being said about your company online. Ideally, you can also dedicate time to being active on these platforms to see photos or other types of content that don't directly mention your brand or products but are worth replying to. Pop-Tarts have received nearly 50,000 retweets for tweets in which they engaged with customers who tweeted product photos but failed to tag or

Figure 3.1   Example of Taco Bell's #TacoEmojiEngine (Taco Bell, 2015)

 Taco Bell
@tacobell

Did you hear about our #TacoEmojiEngine? Tweet us a
🌮 + any emoji to see what happens.

6:19 PM · Nov 10, 2015 · Twitter for iPhone

121 Retweets   **334** Likes

SOURCE Printed with permission of Taco Bell IP Holder, LLC. The Taco Bell name, logo, and related marks are trademarks of Taco Bell IP Holder, LLC and/or its related companies. Advertising © 2019 Taco Bell IP Holder, LLC.

hashtag the brand. One user mentioned dipping a Pop-Tart in Ranch Dressing, to which Pop-Tarts replied 'This is just disrespectful' (@PopTartsUS, 3:13 pm 20 November 2017)

Hopefully, by now you see just how powerful being a digital savage can be and you will begin to implement these tactics in your business, especially around listening. What good is social media to you if you aren't fully immersing yourself into what's said?

Whenever I present this material in person, I often get asked 'Carlos, what if my brand isn't fun or engaging like Wendy's? I'm

Figure 3.2   Taco Bell views of over 1 billion on Giphy (Giphy, 2019)

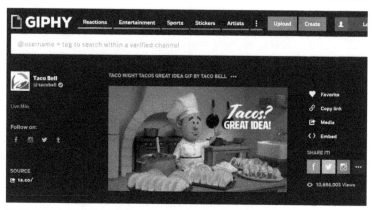

SOURCE Printed with permission of Taco Bell IP Holder, LLC

in a highly regulated industry!' to which my answer 100 per cent of the time goes back to education.

Not every brand can be like Wendy's or Taco Bell or Pop-Tarts – nor should they – but every company can educate through content and real conversations, and ensure that when users are speaking about their company, competition or industry, they are equipped to teach.

For example, consider the brand Ellevest, an investment advisory firm aimed primarily at helping women invest and reach their financial goals. The company started in 2014, led by co-founder and CEO Sallie Krawcheck, who previously held prominent roles at some of the world's largest financial institutions. In just the few years since starting up, the company has amassed an engaged social media community, with more Instagram followers, for example, than some of the world's largest banks and other financial institutions. Ellevest has done so by focusing on creating content that educates its core audience about finance in a relatable way. That includes leveraging Krawcheck to create short, approachable videos answering topical questions in areas ranging from the strength of the US dollar to maternity leave, without being salesy or jargony. The company also creates recurring features such as

#FinancialFeministFridays, where they highlight the stories of inspirational and successful women. That's being on brand and informative without boring their audience with posts touting a new investment fund or only talking about how their platform works.

The key to success for all brands is to be personable and as close to human as possible while working within the confines of a brand logo and guidelines. Although we are at the mercy of the social networks themselves, having a personality (ie, being a digital savage) and following the steps mentioned above centered on community management will help you steal market share away from your competitors and keep people coming your way.

Digital attention is oxygen to keep your brand alive for the time being.

References

Giphy (2019) Giphy search using @TacoBell [Giphy] 4 May [Online] https://giphy.com/tacobell (archived at https://perma.cc/GT6G-62A7) [accessed 4 May 2019]

Taco Bell (2015) #TacoEmojiEngine [Giphy] 10 November [Online] https://giphy.com/gifs/tacobell-taco-tacos-bell-l0NwO6KZuSnJljsQw (archived at https://perma.cc/SP7Q-DVVJ) [accessed 4 May 2019]

Vaynerchuk, G (nd) Gary Vaynerchuk's story [Online] https://www.garyvaynerchuk.com/biography/ (archived at https://perma.cc/AZ92-39KV) [accessed 24 April 2019]

04

Don't be mad at Facebook; you just suck at marketing

At this point, you are a quarter of the way through *The End of Marketing*. As such, I invite you to go to my Facebook page at facebook.com/thecarlosgil and send me a message on what your thoughts are so far.

By now we've covered the state of social media marketing – it's about people, not brands. We've also addressed that your company's online presence is navigating through a digital ocean – it's noisy. And, in the last chapter, I broke down for you how to effectively tap into social media to listen to what's being said and seize market share away from your competition.

Going forward, it's all about tactics and optimization, beginning with Facebook. This chapter is one of the most important of the entire book, so I encourage you to take notes or highlight the steps that I break down for you as points of reference. The material shared in this chapter is often the most popular content that I cover in my conference keynotes; therefore, I know for a fact that you will become a better marketer as a result.

Before writing this chapter, I pondered what life was like before Facebook existed. To be candid, it was less stressful when you could live without having to share what's on your mind or your every moment for validation from strangers.

In 2004 a Harvard student named Mark Zuckerberg created a website that would change the course of history. The social network known as Facebook that we have become familiar with is one of the greatest inventions of all time. I would put Facebook on the same pedestal as the light bulb and the automobile: it's that meaningful. Unlike pioneers MySpace or AOL, Facebook has transformed human civilization, causing us to play out our lives in real time to the extent that the smallest details, such as where we eat, what we enjoy doing, where we go to play or shop, and what we consume digitally can be used by corporations and businesses alike – to sell to us.

Since joining Facebook around 2009, I've shared everything from sombre moments when I've lost jobs to celebrating the births of my children and everything in-between. During this time I've analyzed the psychological effects that Facebook has had on me personally: am I likeable? Why don't more people engage with my content? How come I see the same 20 people's content in my newsfeed? Why don't certain people that I respect and admire in my professional circles ever 'Like' my posts? And, I've spent thousands of dollars on advertising to magically 'cure' the self-inflicted social media blues that Facebook creates. I bet that we've all been there before.

Like most marketers, I have a love/hate relationship with Facebook; however, at the moment it's a necessary evil in all of our lives and for business too.

From 2009 until late 2011, I leveraged Facebook as a channel, no different from LinkedIn or Twitter, to grow my then start-up business JobsDirectUSA, which was an online job board. A key to my success as an inexperienced tech founder was to first connect with professional colleagues and potential clients on LinkedIn and then proceed to become 'friends' on Facebook. By doing so, I now had access to see what these people were like outside of the confines of a professional social network masked by only one photo, which was often a corporate headshot. It was also through the early days of Facebook that I too would share pictures of my young children combined with my professional updates to make myself appear relatable to those watching – a strategy that worked to land me business opportunities. During this time Facebook went through various user interface (UI) iterations including new feature additions such as ads. But the premise back then compared to now was the same: get users to virtually 'like' or follow you and keep them updated with content about you or your business in their newsfeed. Pretty simple, huh? I didn't have a blog or personal website. My Facebook page was my website and so much more – it was a diary.

Then, in January 2012 I was hired by Winn-Dixie – one of the largest supermarket chains in the US – to be their first-ever social media manager. At the time of my hire, there was no social media presence whatsoever, so my first act of duty was to create a Facebook page within 30 days of being hired. Honestly, I had no strategy whatsoever, combined with the fact that I had no team or ad budget. My sole justification for taking Winn-Dixie onto Facebook was that our competition had a Facebook page. Therefore, we needed one too. If you work for a corporation today that has a Facebook page created in the early 2010s and see little to no engagement, it's highly likely that you inherited the mess that I'm about to explain.

Creating a social media presence for a corporation has always been a difficult task. In those early days, those in the newly created social media roles were met with internal skepticism at every turn – often coming from public relations teams and agencies that feared that social was opening up a channel for customers and critics to blast the company. Then, human resources departments became terrified that disgruntled employees would also take to Facebook.

During these early days, while working at Winn-Dixie I created a Facebook profile and Twitter account named 'Winn-Dixie Carlos' or @WinnDixieCarlos (it's still active!). Every day was a struggle, but I was finally able to get buy-in from our vice president of communications (who was my boss at the time) as well as our chief marketing officer, so away to the races we went. The first step was to communicate to thousands of employees that we were now on Facebook, which drove an initial push of fans. Part of my job was to be an internal evangelist for all things social media so I convinced my boss to pay for shirts that said 'Follow Winn-Dixie on Facebook' with our URL, and distributed them to around 800 employees at headquarters during lunch one day. Then, we sent out poster-size flyers to all 1,000+ stores and the 'likes' came in.

Working with our agency lead Nick Cicero, our strategy to gain users was centered on giveaways and promotions. Around this time, circa 2012, Facebook promotions were everywhere (eg, 'Like our page to be entered for a chance to win') and they worked to get a quick, cheap 'Like'. But here's the problem: like many brands we were acquiring followers who weren't interested in our content or being part of our community. They were only there because they wanted to win something. As time went on, we partnered with big consumer packaged goods (CPG) brands like PepsiCo and Coca-Cola, which brought prize assets our way. In two years, we gave away everything from free groceries for a year to Super Bowl tickets to even giving away a Ford pickup truck. Growing to 100,000+ 'likes' seemed like a résumé piece to brag about, and back then, it was. But now, the reality is that only a small fraction of Winn-Dixie's current 240,000+ Facebook followers even see the brand's content. According to the public analytics, less than 20 people on average engage with the brand's organic posts.

Don't hate Facebook – get better at marketing

Please do not be offended by what I'm about to say – most people who work in marketing do not know marketing, and they are not marketers, they're 'content pushers'.

Most marketers today blame their woes (including depressed organic reach and engagement) on Facebook, when it's not Mark Zuckerberg's or the platform's fault that you suck at marketing. I used to think in those days that I was a good marketer, but I wasn't. I was all about the vanity metrics because they looked good, when in reality it wasn't driving much value to the brand.

To be a marketer today requires a deep understanding of how marketing is done, which means diving deep into the platforms and understanding how they work. A common theme that I have seen repeatedly throughout the years by attending industry conferences is how many people who claim to be marketing professionals don't honestly know how social media works because they are not adopters. It's one thing to understand the basics, and it's another to be personally engaged with these platforms, and it's yet another to know how to monetize your brand through social media.

Ever since Mark Zuckerberg testified in front of US Congress in 2018 because of the Cambridge Analytica data scandal, Facebook has been under fire. In an industry group that I run on Facebook called 'Social Media Masterminds Group', many of my colleagues were claiming that Facebook would die and eventually succumb to the same fate as its predecessors AOL and MySpace – but I think that's laughable.

Even with the public pressure the platform faces and no matter how much you might hate the fact that Facebook is making it harder for brands to claim organic reach and monetize, it's not going away.

Facebook is the world's most powerful marketing tool. When leveraged properly, it's more powerful than even Google. The key however is knowing how to maximize the reach that Facebook gives you both for free and with paid spend, and you need to adapt your strategies accordingly.

'In the past on social, people were just creating a bunch of content for the sake of creating content. Nowadays, businesses and brands really should be thinking in terms of campaigns. And strategically, when you're going to leverage paid social, think about how that paid campaign goes to the overarching funnel that you may have and where along the customer journey you are trying to hit them at', says Tyler Anderson, Founder and CEO of social media marketing agency Casual Fridays, co-founder of Tack, and executive producer of Social Media Day San Diego. 'In the past, where brands had to create all this content, now you can create little content – you can literally create 70% less content, but with the right paid strategy, you can still achieve more significant results than when you were creating tons of content.'

Understanding Facebook's algorithm

With over 2 billion active monthly users on Facebook (Facebook, 2019a) and another 1 billion monthly actives on Instagram (Instagram, nd), which they own, Facebook is at the epicenter of social media networking for today's digitally engaged, always-on consumer. Whether your brand is B2B or B2C, Facebook offers marketers the opportunity to reach real buyers, unlike any other existing social network. However, Facebook is a business and increasingly is making it challenging for others to grow their customer base and revenue – for free.

Since the beginning of 2018, Facebook has made it publicly known that it would begin to limit content from brand pages, and it has. Today, less than 1 per cent of brand page fans see content from a page that they had previously 'liked'.

While defeating the Facebook algorithm is virtually impossible, understanding how Facebook prioritizes what content it is serving your customers and thus adapting your social media strategy to what Facebook is most likely to show in users' timelines is vital.

So how does the Facebook algorithm work?

Based on research and a lot of A/B testing, the following types of posts are more likely to appear in one's Facebook newsfeed.

Content from friends, family and groups

It's no secret that you are more likely to see content posted by your circle of friends and network connections before that of a brand. Why is that, you might be asking? For starters, Facebook does not allow for an individual to run ads targeting their friends, but they do for brands. In the first quarter of 2019 alone, Facebook made nearly $15 billion in advertising revenue (Facebook, 2019b). It's big business, which is why it's difficult these days for brands to get free eyeballs on their content. Now that you understand this, keep an eye out for content from Facebook Groups such as my

'Social Media Masterminds Group'. As of now, groups are still the last frontier for 'free engagement' mainly because they are peer-to-peer communities until brands wise up (and they will) by creating their own groups.

Posts that ignite conversation

Stop selling and start socializing. Seriously. We've already addressed that people don't want to be sold to. They prefer to be engaged, therefore begin with speaking to your community by asking them questions that will start a conversation on your page. From something as simple as 'How was your weekend?' to 'How does our brand play into your life?', if you ask open-ended questions on Facebook, you're likely to catch someone's attention and get them to comment, which takes me to my next tip.

Posts with a lot of likes, comments and shares

The mysterious Facebook algorithm is an AI, which can auto-detect and filter out content based on keywords and also engagement actions, which is why your goal should be to get as much engagement as possible within the first hour of your post going live. That means keeping an eye open as those likes and comments come in and immediately replying within the comments of a post to show the algorithm that the post is active and relevant to your intended audience. It's not rocket science, but there is a science to the madness.

Content that keeps users on Facebook

This callout is for the brands that are continually trying to get free website clicks from their Facebook page, as well as YouTube creators who are trying to tap into Facebook to drive potential new subscribers over to their channel. Like any other business, Facebook wants its users to stick around as long as possible because the longer you and your fans are on Facebook, the higher likelihood they have of serving ads to those users. So if you're driving those fans away from Facebook, the algorithm is automatically going to de-prioritize your content. You are going to have to stop posting links to your website, YouTube videos and blog posts, whether it's coming from your personal or your brand page, to keep Facebook happy.

This point is a tough pill to swallow for most marketers and business operators whose sole job is to drive website clicks and revenue through Facebook posts. However, there are alternative methods to be aware of. For example, instead of posting a link to your latest blog post use Facebook Notes. This untapped feature that Facebook offers to all pages can be used to share blog content natively within Facebook, so you can still get your message across and establish yourself as a thought leader. Or, if you have an e-commerce store and thus are trying to drive online sales, try using Facebook's built-in tools for Shopify and e-commerce whereby you can sell goods directly from your page.

Native video content uploads

Facebook is making a play to compete head-on with YouTube and be where you go for all things social networking and media consumption. That's why they now have a 'Facebook Watch' section on the platform, centered on video. Whether you're a personal brand, a creator or a business, create short and catchy video tutorials about what you do to engage users to stick around and watch. Keep in mind that the average user is scrolling fast through their feed, so your video should be eye-catching in the newsfeed with a designed thumbnail, and it should captivate the end user within the first few seconds.

Uploading native video content rather than sending someone to your YouTube channel also helps you keep users on Facebook, as the previous point explains, and you can begin building up data and analytics around viewing history, which is a key metric you can then use to advertise against.

Live video content including real-time tutorials and conference keynotes

If you're in B2B, it's likely that you fall into one, if not all, of these categories: you push out technical white papers to drive lead generation, you attend industry conferences as a speaker or exhibitor, and you have your own partner or customer conference. These assets/activities can be leveraged on Facebook Live, a platform to engage your audience through real-time video where you can do live Q&A or bring your customers into an experience that they can only encounter by tuning in. Think about using Facebook Live the next time you launch a white paper. Try sending out an email blast and invite your customers and prospects to join you at a scheduled time for live Q&A.

During my days running social media at BMC Software and then working with DocuSign through my company Gil Media Co., we leveraged the Facebook Live API to stream the conference keynotes from our user conferences with professional cameras and a tool called 'Open Broadcaster Software' or OBS. Imagine having an actual announcement broadcast live on your Facebook page. Now, imagine that when you go live, those that 'like' your page are made aware of that via a notification on their Facebook app. That is the benefit of going live!

Now, if you're a B2C company, the possibilities are endless when it comes to Facebook Live, from live product demonstrations hosted by employees, customers or influencers, to creating a series like 'A day in the life' centered on your employees.

Types of content to avoid posting on Facebook

Overly promotional content

Once again, Facebook is a business with its primary objective being to monetize brands' access to their communities of users. If your content is overtly selling, such as creating an organic post that asks users to sign up for a subscription to your service, you are likely to be penalized. Instead of using Facebook to try selling directly, get creative – which is the job of a marketer – and ask yourself 'What would I want to see as a customer of my brand?' Better yet, if you really want to know what your community wants, simply ask them in a post.

'Engagement bait' posts

A classic marketing move is to add a call to action in just about every post on social media ranging from 'Click here' to 'Watch this' to 'Learn more' to 'Sign up now'. Facebook can auto-detect when you are intentionally bypassing their ad products, which are designed to help you accomplish your lead generation objective. Therefore, stop using calls to action in your organic posts immediately and instead aim to make your posts more conversational in nature, which will give you a modest engagement boost.

Clickbait or 'fake news'

Clickbait articles and fake news often go hand in hand, such as those ads you see at the bottom of an article touting a secret trick to weight loss 'that scientists are hiding from the public', celebrities who 'faked their own death' or anything else that's eye-catching. Facebook is cracking down on these posts that bait people into clicking on links, including content that's misleading and spammy, such as a caption that reads 'GET YOUR FREE COPY! JUST PAY $19.99 IN PROCESSING!'

Long-form text posts

Your Facebook page is not a blog; however, you do have the ability to create blog-style content within the Facebook Notes feature. Within your main page, however, keep content short. A mistake that I see many make, even on their personal profiles, is they treat a post as if it were an essay; therefore it's difficult if you're reading on a smartphone to follow along. After a while, your eyes wander and you lose interest. My recommendation is to keep your caption short and limit it to two sentences at the most. An old boss who was a pro at writing digital ad copy used to tell me that the key to writing social media copy is to treat it with the succinctness of ad copy: state the takeaway up front within the first sentence.

Excessively tagging others

The last no-no is around tagging other users for the sake of getting a cheap boost in engagement by having your content seen on someone else's page or profile. Don't tag up to 99 users in a post for the sake of maximizing your reach. There's a difference between growth hacking and spamming. All it takes is for one person tagged to report your post as abuse, and the entire post will be removed.

How to growth hack your Facebook content

Now that you know the dos and don'ts of working within the confines of the Facebook algorithm for the best chance of reclaiming organic reach, you can focus on ways to growth hack your reach. That means experimenting with low-cost tactics to see what sticks for your brand, rather than blasting out overly advertised content that doesn't apply to your audience, ie, create spam.

Comment on old posts to trick the Facebook algorithm into thinking it's new

Do you know what Facebook loves? A lot of engagement on a single post because if a piece of content is perceived to be 'viral', it's going to keep people on the platform. My recommendation is that you go back into your archives by accessing Facebook analytics, and find your top-performing content from the last 12 months. Once a week, go into one of your top-performing posts from the past – I refer to these posts as your 'golden oldies' – and 'like' every comment on that post, as well as commenting back. By doing this, that post will now circulate back atop the newsfeed since it has new engagement. Also, followers who are new to your page will now see a piece of content that they haven't seen before.

Boost native video content

Get into the habit of posting native video content on your Facebook page and immediately boost it with a (minimum) $10 ad spend for the first 24 to 48 hours, to give your video a bump in video views and reach. People are more likely to see video content that has thousands of views versus one that has under a hundred, so you need to be willing to add a little fuel to the fire.

Distribute Facebook Ads to third-party partners to expand your reach

Facebook has partnerships with distribution partners such as media outlets and trade publications; therefore, as you're building out your Facebook Ads, be sure to select the option for Facebook to distribute your ad on partner sites. This tactic is a way to get your content seen, and in front of a targeted audience outside of Facebook.com or the mobile app. Also, try distributing your ads to Instagram to reach an audience that might not be paying attention to your brand or following your brand on Facebook.

Build custom audiences with CRM/email lists and build audiences targeting competitors as well as employees

The key to Facebook Ads is to be targeted rather than throwing money away and seeing what works. Most companies have a CRM or email list of some kind. If you do, and if you're able to stay within data privacy regulations, go to Facebook Ads and upload your email list as a custom audience. Now, you can run Facebook

Ads targeting customers who already receive email marketing from you, assuming you're following appropriate privacy guidelines. This tactic will ensure that not only are customers seeing you in their email inbox but on their iPhone or desktop through Facebook as well, assuming again that you're following proper privacy guidelines and can re-target your audience. Once you've uploaded your email data into Facebook, begin to build custom audience segments, which target Facebook users that 'like' your competitors. Take Facebook Ad targeting to the next level by creating segments targeting employees of your company and that of your competition too, so that you can expand your reach.

Create a dedicated group for 'super fans' and enthusiasts

As I stated before, Facebook Groups seem to be the last frontier of organic engagement these days because they are peer-to-peer groups and require an actual person to set up and moderate the group. However, you can also make a group an 'official' company group by linking your page to it. My recommendation is that you create a Facebook Group for people who use your product(s) and services if you have a dedicated user base. Establish the group as a place for networking, Q&A/support and training but don't make it another place to push your sales agenda. Also, think about starting a small focus group with your most engaged fans.

Add captions to your videos

By adding captions to your videos you're able to engage Facebook users who might otherwise skip your video altogether if the volume is off on their iPhone or computer. Also, the main reason you should add captions is because they have precious metadata and keywords within them; when you're competing against an AI algorithm it helps to have these detectable keywords in your video content. Personally, I use Rev.com to create captions for most of my videos.

Set up a Messenger auto-reply bot

The last growth hack is centered on creating an auto-reply bot, which will automatically respond to all enquiries that come to your page whenever someone clicks on the 'Send Message' button, provided that you have it turned on. Setting up a Messenger bot on a page (where you're an admin) takes less than a minute to do. Begin by going to 'Settings' from your Facebook page and then select 'Messaging' on the left-hand side of the screen. From there you can head to the 'Response Assistant' section and create the chat flow experience for your customers, such as starting with a simple 'thank you' message, letting your audience know that someone will respond in detail within the next 24 hours. Keep in mind that there are far more advanced ways of using bots, but this is a free, easy solution to ensure that while you're away from your page, anyone messaging your brand page won't feel ignored. Plus, an auto-reply assistant can help you book appointments and even drive someone back to your website, which we know is important.

Create content that converts

Coming up with ideas on where or how to create content can always be a challenge, so in the points below I address how to create content that converts.

Content leads to a conversation, which leads to clicks

It's likely you're asking yourself at what point, if any, will you send users that 'like' your page back to your website? What you should strive for is to have users commenting on your posts. This is good. When someone comments on your page it will appear in the timeline of your users' friends of friends that he/she left a comment. What you should do immediately after someone leaves a comment is 'like' their comment, comment back by saying thank you or a few words of appreciation, and then drop a link in the reply for them to visit your website.

Where to find possible content to post

You don't have to go too far to find content. Does your Facebook page accept reviews or testimonials? If so, turn these reviews into quote cards, which you can create with a template on Canva.com. There's also employee and customer user-generated content too. And, don't forget that your blog posts, which you're likely sharing to Medium, LinkedIn or your website, can be repurposed on Facebook Notes.

Take up maximum real estate in the newsfeed

As you're creating video content for your next Facebook post, consider creating a vertical (portrait) video similar to what you'd see on Snapchat or Instagram Stories. By default, most Facebook video content is displayed horizontally or in widescreen mode; however, when you post a vertical video, you can occupy more space in the newsfeed when content is viewed on a smartphone. As a reminder, always post native video content with a one- or two-sentence caption versus posting a link to your YouTube channel.

Conducting an audit of your Facebook pages

In conclusion to this chapter, I recommend that you do an audit on all the Facebook pages that you manage before putting into motion any of the tips or strategies mentioned above.

The audit template below is what I use with clients and also present in workshops. Answer each of the following questions:

- What is your purpose for being on Facebook?
- What are your KPIs? (Note: KPIs are measured as clicks, engagements and $ ROI.)
- Who are you trying to reach?
- What type(s) of content are you putting in front of your followers?
- How often are you posting on Facebook?
- How often are you engaging your followers one to one?
- Are you repurposing content from other platforms?
- Are you running ads and if so, how often?
- What were your most engaging posts in the last 12 months?

Each of the questions above should serve as a guide for you and your team to operate, moving forward.

As we wrap up this chapter, I hope that you feel more confident about using Facebook in your marketing mix. Dominating Facebook and any other social network begins with having a strategy, which is why I often ask clients 'Who are you trying to reach and why?' If you can't answer that question succinctly, you should re-evaluate what purpose social media is intended to have in your business. Again, this is a time-consuming endeavor, and it's a shame to waste your time when you might be better suited to using other tactics to grow your business.

Next, as you evaluate possible use cases for Facebook Live, I want you to think about going outside of the box and creating a series similar to a podcast or a vlog, but one that will give users an inner glimpse of what it's like to work at your organization. Better yet, recruit die-hard advocates of your brand to do the content creation for you. Then, build buzz around your content. You can schedule a Facebook Live up to seven days in advance as an event whereby users can request to be notified when you go live.

Take advantage of this feature and promote your live video content ahead of time so when the moment comes to go live it doesn't come as a surprise to your community. Also, cross-promote the hell out of your Facebook Live on other channels as well as including it in your email newsletter.

Speaking of your email newsletter, I would be willing to bet that you have customers right now that receive the weekly newsletter who probably don't follow you on Facebook, which is why from time to time you need to remind your CRM database that you exist on Facebook, via Facebook Ads and callouts in your email newsletter.

By reading this chapter, I also think some marketers will get curious about Facebook Groups and will start a new wave of groups for their companies. Before you run out and start one, instead of labelling your group 'Fans of XX' make the group title appeal to a broader audience or industry. I previously spoke at a conference where I provided this tip and later learned that a boat dealership started a Facebook group called 'Boat lovers', which quickly grew. Creating these communities allows brands to establish their credibility in their fields, without having to be overly promotional.

Last but not least, I can't emphasize enough how important it is to refrain from using Facebook as a place for quick ROI because doing this will not lead to success in the long run. Don't ask for engagement; pay for it. Don't drive people away from Facebook; keep them on your page. I often compare Facebook to a giant flea market, where brands and businesses have booths set up (their pages) and by spending a little bit of money on advertising they're able to recoup their costs and make some profit.

I encourage you to be a savage all day, but you also need to know how the game is played if you want to have a shot at winning it. That's real talk.

References

Facebook (2019a) Stats, 31 March [Online] https://newsroom.fb.com/company-info/ (archived athttps://perma.cc/S5K9-2ZMP) [accessed 24 April 2019]

Facebook (2019b) Facebook reports first quarter 2019 results, April 24 [Online] https://investor.fb.com/investor-news/press-release-details/2019/Facebook-Reports-First-Quarter-2019-Results/default.aspx (archived at https://perma.cc/P6C7-B9AT) [accessed 24 April 2019]

Instagram (nd) Instagram Statistics [Online] https://instagram-press.com/our-story/ (archived at https://perma.cc/M4NK-ZVZM) [accessed 24 April 2019]

05
Swipe right

Sales and marketing is no different from finding your match on Tinder

Much of what you see online today – whether posted by a corporate or personal brand – is intended to make you react in some way. In the marketing world, and also in the 'real world' as everyday users, the reason why we thrive off an engagement is that it represents validation.

Social media is more about understanding psychology and human emotion and less about traditional sales and marketing, which is why I go back to the first line in this book – 'marketing, as we know it, is dead.'

If I create a personal brand persona and get you to follow me because I speak like you, share similar interests, and engage back when you comment on my posts, there's a higher likelihood that when I suddenly drop a video or piece of content promoting a brand, you will take my endorsement as gospel. That in itself is personal branding, and it's also the reason why for many Generation Z and Millennials YouTube has created a platform for creators to share their daily life and get paid for it.

Although brands will occasionally hire an influencer for a quick endorsement and spike in social media engagement, businesses struggle mightily with the concept of making a person or persons the faces of their companies online, because at the end of the day they value the logo over a human face. However, who has more influence today: the logo or the face?

The 'secret sauce' isn't in the content; it's in the personality.

I learned this first-hand between 2014 and 2016, when my career took off in unprecedented ways thanks largely to Snapchat. Through using this platform, I learned about storytelling and this concept of 'humanization of content'. However, I credit the success and limited 'fame' less to Snapchat itself and more to the power of building community.

Throughout 2014 I started analysing the inner workings of Snapchat and also started my YouTube vlog at youtube.com/carlosgiltv. If you go to my YouTube channel and find my oldest video from May 2014, you will see a much younger version of myself in New York for my childhood best friend's wedding. The whole concept of creating my own reality show and sharing it with the 'world' was fascinating and also helped me evolve my brand from being just another face in Twitter chats to a live person – or personality. However, it wasn't perfect. Although to my credit, most people are not naturally good storytellers. Despite creating over 100 vlogs in my first year on YouTube, I wasn't getting thousands let alone millions of views. My early vlogs would get fewer than 100 views on average. In addition to low view counts, I also found myself feeling weirded out by being in public with a camera in hand and having people stare at me. So, I gave up on YouTube altogether – for the time being.

What I wish I had realized then, and what marketers should still keep in mind today, is that creating great content and building up an audience requires patience and perseverance.

On a recent episode of my Nasdaq show *Real Talk*, I spoke with Greg Galant, CEO and Co-Founder of Sawhorse Media, and he shared important advice for new content creators: 'Your content is going to suck at the beginning. It takes a long time to get really good at creating good content' for most people, he said. 'Don't get discouraged at the start' and don't get caught up in comparisons because another creator might have been honing their content for years, so give yourself time to get to that level. 'A lot of great content creation just comes from practice and honing your skill and putting stuff out there, seeing what works with an audience and what doesn't and doubling down on that.'

Similarly, professional YouTuber and podcaster Sara Dietschy also shared on *Real Talk* the importance of sticking with content creation. 'You can't give up. You can't put out one or two videos' and assume people don't like your content, she said. 'I think that's why it's so important to do something you're passionate about. It's cliché, but if you're not passionate about it you're not going to stick with it.'

By sticking with content creation, you can also build up a valuable database of content that adds value once you eventually do attract an audience.

'If you want to have a lasting impact in whatever world you're in, you have to set yourself up for that', said Dietschy. For her, that meant that when she created a video that went viral in 2016, she had a backlog of content so when people found her, they had a reason to stick around rather than moving on to the next sensation. 'I had a lot of good, unique content on my channel that made them stay, that was highlighting the creative process. It was educational but it was inspirational as well. So I think you have to be continually looking for those opportunities to maybe get that viral hit or get that searchable content so people will find you but you have to make sure you're putting in the work and being your unique self to where when people discover you they're going to stay.'

The start of Snapchat

While I was trying to find my voice on YouTube, I spent most of 2014 studying Snapchat and became fascinated by the infrastructure. Although the public-facing Snapchat Stories feature had not been introduced, and Snapchat was strictly a person-to-person messaging app at this time, the fact that I could send someone a video message with my face and voice was exhilarating. Honestly, Snapchat offered a dopamine rush that no other social network at the time provided, since at this point social networks primarily allowed you to publish text and photo-based posts with limited video capabilities. Live video on social media did not exist either.

Another key feature which Snapchat introduced was the ability to see if someone had viewed your message. As an end user I found this feature to be game-changing because now I could tell if someone had opened my video message and was putting me off or ignoring me. Again, a lot of what we encounter on social media is psychologically/emotionally based. I can't tell you how many times I have felt ignored and down emotionally because someone read my message and didn't reply. Today, you can see if someone has opened up your message on Instagram and Facebook Messenger too. Last, and perhaps the main reason why I opted to give Snapchat a try as a then 30-year-old marketing professional trying to become a storyteller, was the fact that I could ditch the point-and-shoot camera and instead use my iPhone, which felt more natural to use in public.

Turn the calendar to the beginning of January 2015, and I was a storyteller on the hunt for a job; 2015 became a defining era for me. I was newly unemployed, so the first thing that I did was send an email out to thousands of LinkedIn contacts informing them of my employment status, which immediately led to a flood of people offering to help. One of those individuals was Travis Wright, who suggested that I create a 'Hire Carlos' Facebook page in lieu of sending out a traditional résumé to potential employers, and as a social experiment he would pay out of his own pocket to run Facebook ads targeting recruiters who worked for the companies that I was interested in working for. Pretty brilliant, huh?

In addition to creating a 'Hire Carlos' Facebook page, I decided to give YouTube a try once more with a renewed purpose of vlogging about what it's like to be unemployed and to connect with others more personally. While unemployed, I 'Carlos Gil' was the product that I was selling, with my approach being to humanize the job search process. If I could get enough people to like and believe in me genuinely, then those individuals would feel compelled to talk about me to their colleagues and network connections. It's no different from what we do today with creating advocates out of our employees and customers.

Although I was actively creating content at various conferences that I was attending, content alone was not the key – my human persona was. I firmly believe that you always need to be fine-tuning your approach to how you find customers and connections on social media by tapping into their human emotions and building meaningful relationships one by one through direct dialogue.

Everything came together during a trip to the Bay Area around February of 2015. First, I interviewed for a job which ultimately, I wasn't hired for. However, I video blogged about the experience of going to the interview in a vlog, which you can find on my YouTube channel, called 'How to Prepare for a Job Interview'. After this, I went over to Oakland for a different job interview, before sticking around in San Francisco to attend a brand innovation summit. Somewhere in-between my interview and the summit I decided that I needed to get a haircut, so I grabbed a shared Uber pool ride and met a woman sitting beside me in the Uber. She asked what I was in town for, which led to me explaining that I was there for a job interview and that I work in social media, to which she replied that she worked as a recruiter for a social network called 'LinkedIn'.

I couldn't make this up even if I tried. If you want to see how serendipity works, go watch the videos titled 'How I Found a Job in an Uber' and 'There's No Quit in Hustle!' on my YouTube channel.

Upon my return home I emailed the woman in the Uber the YouTube videos that I had been creating about job hunting, along with my résumé. The following week I was back on a plane to San Francisco where I interviewed with and was soon hired by LinkedIn. This experience demonstrates one of the ways building a personal brand can bring value, and it also shows how offline and online connections and personas can intertwine.

Even while working at LinkedIn, I kept building my personal brand. At this time in early 2015, Snapchat continued to pick up popularity among Millennials, so I planted my flag in Snapchat and tripled down on content creation there versus YouTube. I like to pride myself that besides maybe Gary Vaynerchuk, I was one of

Figure 5.1 My YouTube Channel videos, including the one documenting how I got the job at LinkedIn (Gil, 2015)

the first marketers to actively adopt Snapchat into my personal brand's arsenal of social networks. I began to save my Snapchat Stories each day and would repurpose them on YouTube, which by doing so helped me gain a bump in Snapchat followers through the YouTube community. Speaking of YouTube, since I was now daily vlogging on Snapchat I began to use YouTube as a tool to teach. No longer were my videos about 'A day in the life of Carlos Gil' but rather the content became grounded in teaching others how to become better marketers by showing the ins and outs of Snapchat for business.

Being one of the first marketers on Snapchat not only meant that I'd have an early start to capture or 'land grab' the attention of Snapchat's community of users but it also meant that I would be one of the first to teach about Snapchat as a marketing tool on YouTube and at conferences.

In fact, I found that I could use Snapchat to grow my personal brand even as my employment status continued to change (my stint at LinkedIn was short, and I moved on to BMC Software in late July). Every day I would hop onto Snapchat and begin my daily story by saying 'What up Snapchat fam!' in an animated, larger than life sort of way. As time went on, I discovered that the key to storytelling on Snapchat – and today everywhere else – became more about me connecting with followers on an emotional level more so than anything I was going to share with you that day. If from the first snap of the day you're seeing me upbeat and full of emotion then it's likely you're going to come back for more. Now, for me as a content creator, it was all about that hit of dopamine, which came in the form of engagement.

Back to Snapchat, as my popularity grew on the platform so did my awareness that I was connecting with people on a level that no other social network at the time facilitated – short, hyper-engaging stories meant to keep people coming back for more. However, the beauty of Snapchat is that only I could see the view counts, which I credit to making me a better storyteller in the long run. The reason why a lot of people give up on YouTube or even Facebook is because they put out content to the world, the material isn't seen by many and that low view number is public, and the person feels like a failure in the process. Conversely, on Snapchat and now on Instagram Stories only you – the end user – can see a view count number. I firmly believe that when only you have access to your viewership data you will produce better content because it's a real challenge that means something to you and nobody else.

Moreover, it's important to have intrinsic motivation to create content, rather than just being driven by people seeing how many views you have.

If you're trying to build a brand and/or become an influencer, 'it can't be about the followers or the fame', said Gerard Adams, an entrepreneur and host of the online show *Leaders Create Leaders*. 'It has to be because you truly want to make an impact on the world. You have a story to tell, you have things you've overcome, you have a real expertise and passion for things in the world.'

Creators can make that impact by opening up to audiences, and it's important for brands to understand that social media users increasingly want to consume content that's real and inspirational, not just in terms of highlighting successes but also failures.

'We all have a gift', adds Adams. 'Once you're able to really tap into that gift, tap into your true story, your true vulnerability, and really tap into why you want to build influence, because it's not about you anymore, you want to serve.'

Don't overly rely on platforms

Focusing on sharing your stories and serving others rather than trying to get as much of a following as possible on one platform is also important because you can then take that message to other media as social media networks change.

In my own case, eventually 'What up Snapchat fam!' ran its course. Snapchat decided to alter the algorithm thus affecting my ability to reach the same level of users as I had before, and I lost my interest in Snapchat. Attempting to recreate the success on Instagram, I quickly discovered that Instagram was already overly saturated with noise and standing out on that platform alone would be difficult at best. Instead, I found success across multiple platforms by sharing different parts of my personal life and my work depending on the audience on each network, rather than being limited to one persona on one network. That's why I often tell friends of mine in the industry who are content creators never to become married to a single platform, and be flexible in building their brands across various social networks.

Recently, I attended Social Media Marketing World – the annual mega-conference, which brings together thousands of marketing professionals including creatives and people who use social media in their businesses. As I shared with countless colleagues, the social networks that we are doing business on are what I call 'rented land'. In other words, you're trying to grow your business on top of an already established company, which is a scary thought when you stop and consider: what if that business goes away or dramatically changes the way they operate?

'Too many people are relying on the platforms in order to determine their level of success. And when you do that you're only as good as what the platform can do for you', said talk show host and NBC's *Today Show* contributor Mario Armstrong, in a recent episode I hosted of Nasdaq's *Real Talk*.

Instead of being limited by the confines of social networks, marketers need to focus on this book's key themes of 'humanization' and 'personification' of content, because those qualities are independent of specific social networks and can easily be transferred to other forms of marketing.

Once you stop giving the social networks all the glory for building up your business and you own the fact that your human ability to pull people in by being 'you' is when you'll realize these platforms are just distribution channels to amplify your voice.

The channels are just that – channels.

So how do you keep people tuned in versus tuning out, no different from flipping the dial on the radio or TV remote control?

That question is the problem that I want to help you solve.

Living in a Tinder world

Today is a different era than when TV, radio and print were our primary sources of consuming content and there was more room for slow builds and deep dives. We are now living in a Tinder world, not just in terms of using apps to facilitate dating but in terms of people quickly reacting to what looks appealing to them. If an image or any other type of content doesn't resonate at initial glance, the user moves on to one of the many other options. Today, the visual appeal of your digital content is what sells your product or service.

Allow me to explain.

Think about a time recently that you were scrolling through Facebook, Instagram, LinkedIn or Twitter. Out of a flood of digital noise, what was the first post that grabbed your attention? Think about what made that post stand out individually. Was it the aesthetics of the post maybe?

As humans, we gravitate to eye candy. If not, Reddit – which is a message board – would be more popular with the average digital consumer than Instagram, which is all about visual storytelling and aesthetics, or YouTube that is strictly video content. Analyze what it is about the digital content that pulls you in personally and begin to reverse engineer as you create content for your business.

For example, brands like National Geographic and Patagonia pull in huge audiences on Instagram by sharing beautiful nature photography. Other brands like Nike highlight inspirational stories and draw people in through images of faces that convey a wide range of human emotions.

With your own brand, think about what type of content you're capable of creating that will quickly attract your audience rather than causing them to keep scrolling. For some that might mean beautiful, scenic photos of the places your employees travel to and for others it might be goofy pictures of the people in your office.

Similarly, in cases where you're trying to attract people to written content, you need a killer headline and lead image. Storytelling is still key, but with whatever you choose to create, keep in mind that you first need to quickly hook people before you can tell a full story.

Next, I'll outline key steps in planning your social media posts in a way that optimizes storytelling from start to finish.

Carefully map out your story, aka 'storyboarding'

As I learned first-hand through storytelling on Snapchat followed by vlogging on YouTube, you should always have a beginning, a middle and an end to your stories to keep your community engaged. Have a plan or a storyboard before you start so you can stay on task. For example, a fashion brand could storyboard an Instagram Story that takes the audience from start to finish through how to dress for a job interview. By having clarity on your end, you can more easily convey to the audience what's happening. Because think about it: if someone stumbles across your YouTube channel for instance and begins to watch a few videos with little meaning or context they're probably never going to come back again much less subscribe. The same applies to Stories and Live Video. Whenever you begin documenting your day or experience and hit that record button, you're essentially 'on', so proceed by stating up front what the end user just opted into watching.

The first words that come out of your mouth on any video content should be 'Hey everyone, today I'm doing _____.' In this Tinder world, video view rates typically only last a few seconds, which is why the beginning is critical. From there, keeping your viewers watching through to the end is extremely difficult, which is why you should keep telling your viewers what is going on in each section while also dropping in subtle statements to keep them hooked, such as 'you don't want to miss this!' or 'keep watching until the end for a surprise!' And in order to keep your audience coming back, give them a call to action at the very end such as asking them to subscribe to be notified when your next video is published or asking them to message you with what they thought about your content.

Write short one- or two-sentence captions

Any time you write a social media post, remember to keep it short. One- to two-sentence captions or short tweets tend to work best, because people's attention spans are short. Too many times I see people using Facebook or LinkedIn posts as a de facto blog, and that's a poor strategy. A visually exhausting post on Facebook or LinkedIn appears spammy and reduces the likelihood of it being read. Users tend not to engage with long-form content unless it's on appropriate channels such as built-in features like Facebook Notes and LinkedIn Articles, blogging sites like Medium, or a blog on your own website that you can use to boost your SEO. But when creating content for social media, think about writing succinct captions like this:

> State the problem up front and follow up with the solution, for example:
>
> 'Social media retention sucks! So I have a way to solve it.'

Your goal should be aligned with getting users to view your content, engage with your content, share your content and maybe even click through to your website to buy from your company. Don't put so much emphasis into writing the perfect caption that it takes away from your main content, especially on sites like Instagram, where people are reacting to what you put in front of them visually.

Ask open-ended questions to maximize engagement

Whenever a post has high engagement in terms of comments or replies it instantly hits a level of digital appeal and intrigue, unlike one that just has a high number of likes, because it shows that people are taking the time to write something in response rather than just tapping a button to like the post. If you want to get a spike in comments start asking your community open-ended questions. Knowing that Facebook will penalize you for posting a call to action such as 'watch this video' or 'comment below' you're better served by asking an open-ended question like 'how does this picture make you feel?' or 'what do you recommend?'

Ditch stock photography and replace it with real-life user-generated moments

I honestly don't know how stock imagery companies stay in business much less why brands buy stock photography and slap it on a social media post thinking it's going to drive user engagement. Stop serving people content that they're likely to see in an airline magazine and instead give your social media audience 'realness' in the form of real images, such as ones generated by your employees or customers.

'The new organic in social is through your customers and your employees. While the algorithms have suppressed the content coming from brands, it has not suppressed the content coming from people. And at the end of the day, people make up brands and people make up your customer base', says Tyler Anderson, Founder and CEO of social media marketing agency Casual Fridays, Co-founder of Tack and Executive Producer of Social Media Day San Diego. He continues: 'So definitely having an employee advocacy program, or a user-generated content program or strategy that is basically empowering your employees or customers to become the storytellers for your brand, that is the most impactful thing you can do, and that is how you organically can still achieve success. In addition to that, that organic content is way more engaging, and more impactful and more trustworthy than what you as a brand could create on your own.'

As described in Chapter 3, you can easily run a search on social networks to see what people are saying about your brand. If you find posts about people using or consuming your product, reach out to these individuals and ask them if you can repost their content on your channels. Or you might follow your customers on social media and ask to share some of their content that relates to your brand. Doing so helps convey that humanness and social quality that brings people to these networks in the first place. For example, an accountant that posts a stock image related to wealth won't make as much impact on social media as one that shares a customer's photo of what they bought with their tax refund.

'People trust recommendations from friends and family members more than anything else. And user-generated content is a subtle form of recommendation because social is a review platform', says Anderson. 'And so for most brands, you need to care about user-generated content, you should embrace it and you should have a strategy for it. It's essentially become the new form of organic social. A caveat though is to make sure you get legal permission for it. A lot of brands are not doing this, they just rip people's content off, and that's a huge no-no.'

Marketing is like dating

Circling back around to the title of this chapter, countless friends of mine throughout the years have found success in dating on Tinder, which I think is a lot like marketing. Although Tinder is one of the most shallow and emotionless forms of online dating that exists (since you're largely choosing to engage with someone based on their looks) the comparison to marketing is just that – what looks appealing is what sells.

In a digital ocean where you have a lot of people and brands creating content – in the millions every second – how do you become attractive to your customers?

- By creating digital eye candy, ie, visually appealing, unique content.

- By engaging your customers one-on-one versus one-to-many.

- By being there for your customers when they need you.

- By being confident yet approachable (remember the examples from Wendy's in Chapter 3).

- By personifying your content through people *not* products.

One example of brand that does this well is American Airlines. Despite never meeting a single member of their social media team in person, I honestly feel as if I have an intimate relationship with American Airlines. That's because as a frequent business traveler, there have been numerous instances when I have had a slight change in my plans and have had to send @AmericanAir a direct message on Twitter asking for help in rebooking my flight. In many of these instances they have come through without me having to lift a finger and call customer support, and this ease of communication makes me feel more loyal and connected to the brand.

In fact, marketing and business are very much like dating. Going back to the 'r-word': it's all about the relationship. In business, you're likely to work with someone that appeals to you personally. You trust the person that's selling to you with all of your intimate business needs and secrets, and ultimately you lock into a business relationship with the entity that always over-delivers on their commitment to you and in getting the job done.

Getting to that end stage, however, requires more emphasis on the fine details at the beginning or the middle of a relationship.

Think of sales and marketing as being the same, where the middle of the sales funnel is the marketing content you create to hook your users or prospects.

In business, we are all trying to sell, so the strategy is more about focusing on optimizing your 'marketability', which is what makes you attractive to a potential customer whether it's one person, one thousand or one million. It doesn't make a difference. Ask yourself the following:

- Would I buy from my company? If so, why would I buy from them?
- What are they offering me that is different from the next offer?
- Is the content that I am pushing out creating noise *or* giving immediate value up front?

In terms of giving value up front, I think of people like my friend Roberto Blake who has built a loyal following by giving immense knowledge on visual design and YouTube growth strategies (for free) on his channel to his 200,000+ subscribers. In comparison, there are plenty of self-proclaimed gurus on Facebook that try to pitch 'exclusive', expensive masterclasses without offering anything up front that gets me to trust their expertise.

Giving value up front and offering something unique is similar to the courting process. You can't just ask someone to be in a relationship without first sharing information about yourself and building rapport. And the same way you have to swipe through many prospects and have several intimate conversations on Tinder before you lock in a date is the same way you will have to have many conversations on social media before you convince that one buyer to swipe a credit card, write you a cheque or agree to a cup of coffee.

Think of 'old school rules with new school tools' as the game. In the MySpace days, your profile music was all about telling others what you were into from a music and culture standpoint. Yes, you can tell a lot by a person by what type of music they listen to. Today, although the internet is noisy and cluttered, there are still subtle signs we should be putting out to the digital universe to attract the customer or end user that we want to reel in and engage with our content, such as coming up with a clever Twitter bio and peeling back the curtain into how your brand operates through platforms like Instagram Stories.

To be candid, I wouldn't have the career that I have today and probably wouldn't be writing this book if I hadn't built the persona that I did on Snapchat many years ago, which included sharing vulnerable moments on YouTube and social media during a period where I was unemployed. And, it was through Snapchat that I learned first-hand if you can speak into a 5.8-inch screen in the palm of your hand and get people watching on the other side to like you, then you've captured the one word that brands spend millions of dollars trying to win – attention.

Attention is the commodity. Marketability is the strategy. Likeability is the measurement.

So in closing, how likeable are you? Do your followers and customers want to marry you *or* are they only around until a competitor sweeps them away?

Reference

Gil, C (2015) How I found a job in an Uber, YouTube, 29 January [Online] https://youtu.be/Oo3awOupx-U (archived at https://perma.cc/R7LM-E7FY) [accessed 4 May 2019]

06
Growth hacking your way to greatness

There's a difference between cheating and growth hacking. To 'cheat' in the social media world is to obtain results the easy way, such as by buying followers, and inevitably bypass the hard work that's required to get the same results, which would otherwise take much longer to achieve (ie, organically grow followers, subscribers, et al).

On the other hand, 'growth hacking' is a form of strategy combined with tactics. Happily, it can also help you bypass tedious tasks that take time, money or effort to get the objective you're seeking. Unlike cheating, however, growth hacking requires a deep understanding of the process, the platforms, and experimenting with various tactics through trial and error to obtain the desired outcome.

Although the term 'growth hacker' has become a buzzword in the internet marketing world, growth hacking is not marketing. It's achieving the desired outcome of marketing (ie, get more customers or leads/revenue or raise brand awareness) while being more strategic within the platforms themselves without too much reliance on activities that require ad budget or overhead costs such as employees. Growth hacking also requires a deep understanding of how to phrase content in posts, so it's considered 'algorithm friendly'.

Although the mere thought of cheating or growth hacking your way to the top might make you cringe, the outcomes that they both present are not parallel. Allow me to break down the results in both scenarios so you can see that if you want to stand out online, you need to adopt a growth-hacker mindset immediately:

- If you want to grow your Facebook likes, Instagram or Twitter followers, or YouTube subscribers without having to put in years of labor-intensive work, I can tell you where to buy followers with a couple of keyboard clicks and the stroke of your credit card.

- If you are struggling to get engagement on any of your social media posts, I can tell you where to buy engagement that will ensure your next Instagram post will be seen on the Instagram Explore page.

- If you want to appear in people's notifications while you are sleeping but wake up with hundreds of new followers on Instagram, I can tell you what bot to use and how to program it.

Now, what I just broke down above are cheating tactics, which I do not recommend to anyone. I have toyed around with these tactics, because to teach others how to growth hack, I also need to understand the outcomes of cheating versus growth hacking. So allow me to explain further.

To a certain degree, if you want to understand how this 'game' of social media and internet marketing is played, you must know that a lot of what we all see is 'smoke and mirrors'. Meaning, it's not real. Those follower and engagement numbers don't mean anything if you aren't converting. And as Nick Utton, a marketing expert who has worked as a chief marketing officer at companies such as E-Trade, JPMorgan Chase and MasterCard said on a recent episode of Nasdaq's *Real Talk*, 'Some of the metrics shared by media partners are full of fluff. They're not substantive and quite frankly they look great on a sheet of paper or on a digital imprint... but they do not work.'

The metrics that matter can vary a bit from brand to brand. A non-profit, for instance might care about the overall number of 'likes' if it indicates their mission has growing awareness, but generally revenue and cash flow generated from marketing activities are the main metrics that matter. Yet too many brands fall into the allure of chasing vanity metrics like number of impressions or number of followers.

'Metrics are key, but there's hard metrics and there's a hell of a lot of soft metrics, which are full of BS. And one of the things I pride myself on is being very involved in the media planning and optimization and execution (ie, end-to-end marketing) and make sure that those metrics justify those decisions', said Utton. 'A lot of CMOs are not well-versed in hard metrics and soft metrics and they basically assign these responsibilities to media agencies and media planners and buyers in the company who quite frankly are distant from the true business metrics, and hence decisions are made that are suboptimal.'

Cheating isn't winning

While metrics like revenue and cash flow tend to be the top ones that matter, it's understandable why some brands chase vanity metrics. Instinctively, you are more likely to associate credibility with someone that you see that has a lot of social media followers compared to someone who has, say, fewer than 1,000. Am I right?

Yet I can't tell you how many times in the last 10 years I have met colleagues who have hundreds of thousands of followers on Twitter yet they don't produce content, they aren't outstanding teachers in person and they aren't actually well known. The fictitious number that we call a 'following' is how these individuals, who have purchased followers throughout the years in addition to doing follow-for-follow tactics, remain relevant. What's sad is that we continue to associate digital influence with verified checkmarks – which are often used to identify celebrities' real accounts, but there are ways for far lesser-known individuals to obtain this status – and follower counts that can be gamed and inflated to show the illusion of fame.

As humans, we become so enamored by the thought of being well known and famous that we'll bypass the hard work of growing a dedicated, loyal fanbase in favor of swiping a credit card and buying 'fake followers' or 'bot accounts'. That's not being strategic, it's cheating, and it doesn't work. Why? Because it rarely leads to real engagement or ultimately revenue and cash flow. It doesn't do any good to buy 100,000 fake followers on Twitter or Instagram, only to get fewer than 100 engagements from 'real people'. As well as being ineffective, most users can also quickly identify when someone has purchased fakes. For fun, I will often take a look at certain individuals who purchased 300,000 'likes' on Facebook or 100,000 'followers' on Instagram only to see that they get maybe two or three comments. The aim is to be perceived as famous by your audience, but if nobody engages with your content, it's a sign that nobody is paying attention. In most companies or organizations if you are buying followers and doing follow-for-follow tactics to build up your following and you're not converting; you will eventually have to answer the question of 'Why is our engagement so low?' So, it's best not to do it at all.

Paying homage to 1980s video games, this is called the 'cheat code strategy' of social media marketing. For those of you who grew up on classic Nintendo or Sega Genesis video games, remember when the opening credits of the game would start, you'd immediately mash up a series of buttons to get more lives or skip to the end of certain parts of the game? You weren't becoming a better gamer – what you did was bypass the lessons it took through trial and error to be a better gamer. You cheated to win *Super Mario Brothers* and *Zelda*, but you missed the whole point of actually playing the game.

Growth hacking

While I'm not a fan of cheating, I do encourage being scrappy when appropriate and, more importantly, learning the tricks of the trade to get people's attention. This is where growth hacking comes into play in this game. Unless you work for a company that gives you ungodly amounts of budget to run Facebook Ads and do the 'cool stuff' that's going to go viral, 99 per cent of us have to operate as growth hackers and make things happen. Sometimes you have to zig when others zag, and sometimes you have to take a risk trying something new, with a clear focus on trying marketing tactics that can have an outsized impact compared with what you put in. And as Nick Utton said on the same *Real Talk* episode, it's important to 'fail fast'. In other words, test new tactics and strategies, and if something doesn't work, be willing and able to quickly change course. It's what I have done for the last ten years and will continue to do as social media platforms evolve and introduce new features. Trial and error are what makes me proud to be able to write this book and speak on stages around the world to teach others.

Let me give you an example of growth hacking, which began in late 2008, when I was laid off in the midst of the global financial crisis, and went on until the start of 2015 when I began working at LinkedIn.

When I talked to my mom about my career situation in 2008, she suggested that I joined what was then a lesser-known website called 'LinkedIn' and said that it would be an excellent resource for me. After all, my mom explained that she and my dad, who are real estate brokers, were using LinkedIn to connect with human resources (HR) professionals to assist with the relocation of doctors to Port St. Lucie, Florida, where they (mom and dad) do business. The same day I spoke with my mom about this, I decided to join LinkedIn.

To be candid, I knew nothing about marketing or running a business. But I saw LinkedIn for what it was then and what it is now – a goldmine to reach business executives and decision makers directly related to your career or brand goals.

After signing up for LinkedIn, I came up with a business idea where I could use the newly discovered powers of LinkedIn to gain traction. So, I decided to register the domain for my then website JobsDirectUSA.com, I purchased a job board script and taught myself how to code. It wasn't perfect by any means, but I had a database whereby employers could post jobs (for a fee), and job candidates would be able to create a free profile as well as upload their résumés. Mind you; this was 2008 where the competition in the job board space was sites like Monster.com and CareerBuilder. Later on, Indeed.com would come into the mix, and I found a way to import their jobs via RSS into my website to offer millions of job postings, but that came much later.

Through a lot of A/B testing, trial and error, and deploying aggressive email strategies, I eventually figured out ways to grow awareness for my new business. It's funny because to this day I will meet people who say that they used to get emails from me all the time during my JobsDirectUSA days.

Here's the thing about growth hacking, to be candid: you can't pay any attention to what people say about you; you have to stay focused on your broader objective, and that's what I did.

First, I created a LinkedIn group called 'JobsDirectUSA' followed by LinkedIn groups for seemingly every single major US city (eg, 'Atlanta Jobs', 'Miami Jobs', 'New York Jobs', etc). Because groups are indexed algorithmically on the platforms and search engines too, it's essential that you give them a standard, searchable name. Back then LinkedIn would give you the option to make your group public, whereby anyone could join, or private which required a moderator or group admin to screen potential members and manually approve each one that would participate. Also, LinkedIn gave you the option to send an automated email to users upon request to join your group along with another automated message upon joining – similar to ClickFunnels or any other marketing automation platform that we use today.

Playing within the rules of the game, I realized that I could leverage these features to grow my business. Each of my LinkedIn groups was set up so that you had to request to join, and upon asking to join you would receive an email that came from LinkedIn with a script that read something like this:

> Thank you for requesting to join JobsDirectUSA, one of the largest and most active groups on LinkedIn for job candidates and hiring professionals.

While we review your request to join, please visit www.jobsdirectusa.com to add your resume to our candidate database which is searchable by 1,000s of job recruiters or register to search for resumes posted by qualified professionals and post unlimited jobs.

You want to talk hustle? That was hustle – and it worked.

Then, upon joining the groups new members would receive a follow-up email stating:

Congratulations on joining the group! Upon joining please introduce yourself to the group members.

If you haven't done so already, visit www.jobsdirectusa.com today to sign up as a job seeker or employer and maximize your chances of being discovered.

Because the emails technically came from LinkedIn, I was able to gain more initial legitimacy than I could if I emailed users directly as an unknown entity. In the weeks and months after launching JobsDirectUSA, I was seeing surges of anywhere from 100 to 1,000+ new members joining the website every day. I could then export their email addresses into a CSV file to then import into Constant Contact, which I would then use to sell my services via email, and at that point the audience was more likely to have some familiarity and trust with my brand.

At the time LinkedIn also had a feature whereby you could import email lists into your groups, which would trigger LinkedIn to send an invitation to the email addresses on your list.

Meanwhile, I stayed active on LinkedIn, both in terms of running 20 or so groups of my own, which acted as lead generation and data mines, as well as being a member of the top groups on LinkedIn for HR professionals where every day I would get involved in discussion threads to encourage others to join JobsDirectUSA.com.

At one point I had over 100,000 members registered on my website and close to 1 million email addresses stored, which became the basis for growing my LinkedIn connections, followers on Twitter and friends on Facebook. Any time I saw the opportunity to upload an email list for the purpose of triggering an invitation I took it – and it worked.

Early on I discovered the key lesson that having access to data that you own (versus renting it from a social network) is the play.

Six months after launching my job board, I hosted my first-ever 'Pink Slip Party' in downtown Jacksonville at a martini bar and lounge. Pink Slip Parties were popping up all over the country back then as networking mixers for unemployed professionals to meet and mingle with staffing firms and hiring employers. Planning my first Pink Slip Party not only landed me a feature by CNNMoney ('A job finding people jobs') at the time but it also led to significant news media coverage in my local market, which attracted over 300 people to attend the first event that I ever hosted. So how did I do it? I leveraged Twitter to pitch to local news media that JobsDirectUSA was hosting a free event to help those in the community affected by a layoff become hired. With limited knowledge around public relations (PR), my instincts told me that if a news outlet was on Twitter it was likely someone would be reading on the back-end, so I got to work self-promoting and pitching to news media and the local business community.

Similar to my strategy of creating LinkedIn groups to mine data and grow my following, I took to Facebook to try the same approach of creating a group solely dedicated to the Pink Slip Party movement and unemployed professionals everywhere. I saw a need

Figure 6.1   Example tweet showing how to self-promote a PR piece

Figure 6.2   Example of how to create a value add or excitement when promoting an event

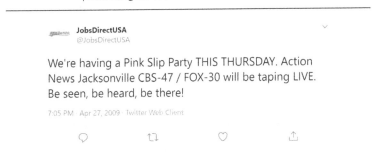

Figure 6.3   Example of how to use Twitter to extend a request or personal invite with a direct call to action

to provide a service that people value and also target a niche audience, so I went after both and did my best to own it.

Eventually, the word about the Pink Slip Parties grew, and the events became bigger. I remember hosting a Pink Slip Party in the middle of the summer in Orlando, Florida, and a line wrapped around the venue before we even opened. People were desperate to find work, and the events provided them with an outlet of hope. Things were moving in the right direction, but 2009 was a sobering year for me nonetheless and a lot of hard work. By the time that the first anniversary of my layoff came around I understood how to growth hack a data gold mine in LinkedIn, I knew how to use Twitter to attract mass media attention to my events, and

Figure 6.4   Example of how to use a call to action across social media platforms, in this case to join a Facebook group

Figure 6.5   Example of how to create engagement using the tease of a follow up being posted at a future date

I discovered that Facebook was virtually untapped as a sales and marketing channel. I had gained so much knowledge, but it required a lot of man hours, sleepless nights and work – which is why I tell people today not to become distracted by shiny objects but rather understand how the platforms truly work so you can get much more out of them besides a cheap follow or engagement.

The real work, however, was in the business that I was building and helping people find jobs. By creating an engaged following, I ultimately started catching the attention of larger businesses, which led to more revenue and cash flow for my business – key metrics that matter. For example, via JobsDirectUSA and my own growing personal brand, I gained Winn-Dixie as a client, for which I promoted job fairs on social media.

Figure 6.6   Example of how I promoted events for my client
at the time

Carlos Gil ✔
@carlosgil83

Winn-Dixie Management Job Fair in Jacksonville, FL on
Wed. 12/8 #hiring #jobs #jacksonville #winndixie
http://bit.ly/dGTlyL

4:58 PM · Dec 4, 2010 · Twitter for Android

Fast-forward to 16 March 2015: it's my first day working at
LinkedIn, and I am in Mountain View, California, (LinkedIn headquarters) for new hire orientation. The same company that I once
leveraged to grow a start-up during the recession is now my employer. As general practice at LinkedIn, as a new hire you have to
introduce yourself to your colleagues and state a little about yourself, along with one thing that you've done that's not on your
LinkedIn profile. On this day LinkedIn's CEO Jeff Weiner was in the
room when I stood up, and I shared how I built a start-up with $0
using LinkedIn groups. Although my employment at LinkedIn was
short, I will for ever be able to claim that my ability to growth hack
their platform not only helped me build a business which put thousands of professionals back to work but it also led me to reinvent
myself in spite of adversity, landing me full circle at a job with the
company itself. Growth hacking is also what led me to get hired by
other big brands such as Winn-Dixie, Save-A-Lot and BMC Software.

All of this growth hacking isn't just relevant for self-employed
business owners who don't have a massive marketing budget. In a
crowded online world, it's increasingly a necessity at a corporate
level too, when you are forced to drive KPIs and business results
without being able to expand resources such as employees or advertising budgets.

The game here is to capture as much attention as you possibly
can with the resources you have. Once you know how the game's

played, then you officially become a player. Whether your objective is to get more video views or capture precious data (ie, email addresses and phone numbers) like I once did on LinkedIn, begin implementing these growth-hacking strategies in your social media marketing mix.

As you learned in Chapter 4, Facebook is Goliath and you are David. You can't expect to easily conquer the platform; instead, you need to focus on growth hacking by understanding the nuances of the network that are relevant for your brand. Think of Facebook like a casino, where small gambles can lead to big payouts (ie, results) and significant risks (ie, running Facebook Ads without discipline) can lead to losing to the house. The good news is that there are a few strategic areas that you can turn to right now to growth hack Facebook and other social media networks.

Facebook Groups

While Facebook Groups don't offer the robust marketing automation capabilities that LinkedIn Groups once offered (and has since removed), you can still use Facebook Groups to grow a qualified audience of potential buyers for your business. The primary reason why I like Facebook Groups is that they seem to be the last frontier on Facebook for organic reach in the newsfeed. Because a group is a digital community that you join, you will begin to receive updates in your newsfeed when others post in the group, even if you aren't technically 'friends' with that person on Facebook.

The critical move with Facebook Groups is to create a sense of community versus being a sales channel, which can be tricky for anyone who is immediately looking to monetize. If you're a niche business of any kind, do your research and see if any Facebook Groups exist for your business or specialty. Assuming your sector isn't oversaturated yet, my recommendation would be to create a Facebook Group that is local and relevant to your community or industry. For example, if you're a real estate agent, form a Facebook Group with a clear, straightforward name such as 'Real Estate

Agents on Facebook'. I'd be less concerned with having my name or likeness associated with the group because your main goal is to get people to join. Once they join you then have easier access to reach them instead of depending on the traditional newsfeed. By having a more generic name, however, you can have relevant keywords in your group title that will organically help the group be discovered through searches on Facebook and via Google. Once you've created your group be sure to set screener questions, which are required for users who request to join. I have personally seen screeners include 'What is your email address?' to 'Your email is required as part of your inclusion in this group' to 'Are you interested in learning more about ___? Drop your email below'. You can customize your screener questions to what fits your group best, and keep in mind the importance of using screeners to vet the members while also gaining valuable data and potentially getting users to take further action such as visiting your website.

If creating a Facebook Group is too much work for you or if there's not a good opportunity to start a new one, join groups relevant to your industry or city where you do business. While you don't want to be overly promotional, there are some opportunities in these groups to pitch your own content lightly. For example, I have not shied away from using other people's Facebook Groups to share links to my online courses, my own Facebook Groups or video content to boost video views. Still, if you have the time and patience to start or join a Facebook group, you need to actually engage and have meaningful dialogue. The most effective way to grow your personal brand is to bring value to these groups by commenting on discussion threads or sharing relevant content that is not self-promotional.

LinkedIn Groups

Staying on the topic of groups, although what you can do as a group owner in LinkedIn Groups has drastically changed over the years, there's still significant value to be gained from joining a LinkedIn Group, such as becoming an indirect connection of the group's members. Meaning, by entering the same group as me you now can message me because we are both parts of the same group. It's a nice workaround (growth hack) without having to rely on LinkedIn Sales Navigator or a premium account to find users relevant to your business. Because LinkedIn allows users to join up to 50 groups, I recommend that you join up to 50 groups that are a mix of industry groups, local groups, and also professional or trade association groups relative to who you are selling to. Throughout 2008– 2011 I was an active member of the most prominent groups on LinkedIn for HR professionals. Same as Facebook, stay on the side of caution when it comes to self-promoting your content but do use these forums as an opportunity to engage in discussions and network. Another growth hack to know about when it comes to using LinkedIn Groups is that most LinkedIn members opt in to receive email notifications, meaning if you start a group discussion there's a likelihood that you can get into someone's email inbox indirectly just because you're in the same group. Any time someone comments on that thread it appear in the email notifications.

Facebook Watch Party

Do you want to know what the secret to going viral is on social media? Get a lot of engagements and views within the first few hours of a piece of content being posted. One way to get that engagement is to host a Facebook Watch Party, which has been a 'secret weapon' of sorts for me since Facebook introduced this feature. It allows a group of viewers to have access to a piece of video content or a playlist of several videos, which you curate. With Facebook Watch Party I have been able to get thousands of video views (for free) on content within an hour of the video being posted. The way it works is that you join groups relevant to your industry that allow Watch Party sharing. For example, if there's a group that has 100,000+ members and has enabled Watch Party sharing, join. Once your video is posted to your Facebook Page go into the groups where you are a member and launch a Watch Party for your video. When you launch a Watch Party, Facebook will notify all of the group members and instantly flood your Watch Party with viewers. Even if those viewers hang around for a few seconds it's considered a view towards your overall view count – and it's free. My only caution is to limit launching Watch Parties to a handful, as Facebook will temporarily ban your account from posting in groups if you abuse this feature.

Native blogging

To this day I don't understand why so many people get caught up in launching their own blog versus using existing built-in resources that vastly improve SEO without having to build up from scratch. LinkedIn has native blogging options for LinkedIn profiles and Facebook business pages can use 'Facebook Notes'. Also, Medium.com is a stellar option if you want to blog without going through the process of manually setting up your own WordPress blog. Through native blogging you are giving the social networks what they desperately want – content. You are also able to benefit by having users read your content within the social network or app and share it to their communities seamlessly. Because you are the author of the content, anyone who comes across it will have the ability to immediately follow or add you without having to click away and go elsewhere. Plus, the SEO benefit of having more links on LinkedIn or Facebook is advantageous.

How to frame content for maximum engagement

What I have learned over the years is the less you say on a post the higher likelihood you have of getting users to watch your video or click through to your website. However, it's all in how you frame your post: keep it open-ended, challenging and conversational.

For example, many of my posts in which I want someone to take action will lead in with a question such as 'Who wants a copy of my new e-book on social media strategies?' A recent post like that, asking my community if they wanted something of perceived value, led to 200+ comments and replies, whereas the day that the e-book launched I also posted the link to the e-book download as a stand-alone piece of content, and it hardly received any engagement. Ask your open-ended audience questions but also lead the horse to water by posting a statement such as 'Curious to hear your thoughts on this video' or 'You won't believe what happened!' or 'I'd love your feedback on how I can improve'. Hopefully, you get the gist of how framing your post to be short yet deliberate is critical. Too many people mess up by treating a Facebook or LinkedIn post as a blog or an ad.

Create Instagram and Twitter pods

The more that you explore the world of growth marketing and growth hacking the more you'll realize that, sadly, many of the internet superstars, celebrities and influencers that we see have grown their following by using some form of trickery, whether it's buying followers or engagement or having their content shared into an engagement pod or all of the above. 'Engagement pods' are private groups within Instagram (up to 20 users) or Twitter (up to 50 users) where whenever a member of the pod posts a piece of content they share it in the pod and the other pod members are supposed to like and comment on the post. By getting a like and comment from other pod members who are likely influencers and have big followings, the original user's post is able to gain reach and get a quick engagement boost, which often results in a post picking up engagement from both accounts that auto-like content posted by influencers or users who see the big engagement numbers and feel compelled to also like and comment. This is a big business whereby agencies, talent agents and brands are looking for the biggest ROI possible measured by impressions and reach instead of dollars.

I am in several Instagram pods that do little for my brand besides getting an occasional 'Nice post!' with a thumbs-up.

However, that's not to say that pods are inherently bad. By curating real communities rather than trying to get likes and comments just for the sake of it, you can boost your marketing effectiveness. For example, I have created pods over the years that I've categorized on Instagram such as 'media', which is where I share selective content to mass media outlets and 'hustlers', which is where I share content to accounts that share quotes, business tips, etc. The most interesting pods I have personally created are what I call 'The Twitter 50'. These are private DM groups where I add 50 random Twitter followers of mine and then sit back and watch them engage with each other. I will share my content selectively when it feels right, without coming off as self-promotional. The most exciting pod I am a member of is one for LinkedIn influencers which, ironically, is hosted on Facebook as a Messenger Group Chat used to share posts from LinkedIn.

Automate engagement with bots

Little by little Twitter and Facebook are cutting off their precious API to platforms that make it possible to growth hack the system, so I would proceed with caution any time you use a tool to automate your engagement. Over the last year, I have actively used a tool called 'Cleaner', which I downloaded from the iOS store to effectively 'clean up' or unfollow Instagram accounts that I had previously followed that either didn't follow me back, were inactive or considered a 'ghost account' meaning they didn't engage with me actively. For years I used a service called ManageFlitter to do the same on Twitter until Twitter cut off their API access. Now, you're probably wondering why it matters who I follow and how many people I support. Well, my mantra on the whole follow-for-follow thing is that if I am following you, but you aren't following me then why am I going to give you my attention? Knowing as a marketer that attention is a currency, I would prefer not to have you take up space in my newsfeed, so instead, I can actively engage with people that are more likely to buy my book, see my content and form a dialogue with me. Now I keep my Instagram feed limited to around 300 or so active people that I follow.

The issue with bots is one that is quite controversial among social media marketers. First, there's a difference between a Facebook Messenger bot that's used to automate customer service responses for brands compared with a bot that auto-comments on Instagram. In full disclosure, I have used various types of auto-engagement bots, such as clean-up ones, for years on both Twitter and Instagram with my justification being that bots help me do the menial tasks that I would otherwise do without a bot, but would take hours of my time to complete. SocialOomph is another automation tool that works to do everything from automating the process of posting content to importing content from RSS feed content into your timeline, which saves a lot of time in finding and scheduling content. If you can find a tool that still works and helps you automate DMs, try it. The key factor is to program your automated DM not to 'right hook' or come off as salesy up front. What you need to do is get the conversation started by saying something along the lines of 'Thank you for following me! What do you do?'

Here's the deal with bots, they can only do what you program them to do in order to save you time. They're no different from when you hire a virtual assistant (VA) or employee to help take tasks off your plate.

You are now halfway done with this book. Hopefully, by now, you've learned how to play the game more craftily (it's about growth hacking, not cheating) while working within the confines of the social networks themselves. Social media can provide you with tremendous power, but it's a big business, which means you are in a competition against millions of other users like you. Remember, if you aren't talking to your customers, most likely someone else is. The premise of this entire book is to teach you that marketing (as we know it) is dead. What worked in the past won't work now. To stay competitive in the game and eventually separate yourself from the pack, you need to be more human and relevant to your intended audience. For inspiration, I suggest watching more of the brands who are taking attention away from you and thinking more about how specific people – whether it's a celebrity, your friend or even yourself – use social media and get engagement, because that is what brands need to emulate moving forward.

07

Marketing lessons from social media giants DJ Khaled and Kim Kardashian West

Today's celebrities are real people on the internet. They too are brands, and the lessons that corporate entities can learn from them are plentiful.

However, I am not a fan of influencer marketing. I think influencer marketing doesn't work for the reasons listed below:

- It's a temporary band-aid to create brand relevance on a short-term basis.

- 'Influencers' aren't really influencing their audiences to buy from a brand. They create a temporary engagement 'boost' by asking their communities to 'like' a post in which the brand client is tagged, thus making it appear that the brand was seen across social media more than the previous day or the day after.

- Many 'influencers' have been known to buy followers and engagement (ie, likes, comments, views, etc) or be members of 'engagement pods' whereby others in the pod will engage with the influencer's post as soon as it's posted in order to give it a 'boost', like a wave that catches momentum before it crashes ashore.

- Influencers' communities are loyal to them, not the brands that pay them for an endorsement. This goes back to the first point – it's a temporary solution, not a long-term strategic play.

Influencer marketing is a lazy and ineffective form of marketing, which does little – if anything – for a brand. To be candid, rarely does influencer marketing work to drive sales. Digital creators who label themselves as 'influencers' are leading brands to believe that they can over-deliver on all sorts of KPIs including sales, when in reality they are gaming the platforms to make it appear as though they are driving real engagement to the brand. As I said in the previous chapter, it's all 'smoke and mirrors'.

If I sound critical of influencer marketing, it's because I am – the truth hurts. However, I want my marketing colleagues that read this to understand that every brand is capable of doing what influencers do. Every brand has access to the same tools as every influencer. There is nothing an influencer does that a brand can't do themselves. Quite frankly, you already have influencers that work for you called 'employees' and influencers who buy from you every day called 'customers'. You, the marketer, can do influencer marketing better than any person that you pay to publicly endorse your company, and in this chapter, I am going to teach you how.

In the early 1990s, there was a show on MTV called *Real World*, which set the stage for what we refer to today as 'reality TV'. The *Real World* was revolutionary because it gave us a glimpse of perceivably everyday people living in a house with no real purpose or agenda. These 'stars' of the *Real World* were not actors or celebrities but benefited by being seen by millions on television. They were in many ways the equivalent of today's YouTube star or 'influencer' on social media. In the decade after *Real World*, we began to see a new wave of reality TV shows from *The Bachelor* to *Big Brother* to *Survivor* and in 2007 the premiere of a now ubiquitous series called *Keeping Up With The Kardashians*. Without the rise of reality TV, we probably wouldn't be enamored with seeing 'normal' people play out their daily lives on Instagram Stories or vlog what they did yesterday on YouTube or pour out their souls on Facebook for the world to consume.

The rise of reality TV and famous 'normal people' means we've also entered the 'reality era of marketing'. This is the intersection where advertising and storytelling meet.

In the early 2000s, if you wanted to have direct access to a celebrity of any kind it was almost impossible unless you knew someone. Then, Twitter changed everything.

For as much love that YouTube and Facebook get as being pioneers, Twitter doesn't get enough credit. Founded in 2006, Twitter created one degree of separation between everyone on the platform – a new level of 'access', which no other social network before or to this day offers. It's a platform where almost every word that is tweeted is made for public consumption and searchable.

The ethos of Twitter being a social network is having content that is short (a 'tweet'), easy to consume, direct and to the point. Searchability being as simple as typing in someone's name or @username, and categories of content being searchable through #hashtags was new at the time and as such caught on with celebrities and their fans. Then came the brands.

With a wildly popular reality TV show in *Keeping Up With The Kardashians* raising her notoriety at the time, media personality and entrepreneur Kim Kardashian West became one of the first notable celebrities to join the ranks of Twitter in March 2009. Today, Kardashian West has over 60 million followers on Twitter and another 133 million followers on Instagram to go along with 29 million 'likes' on Facebook. These audiences are larger than the following of most of the world's largest corporations.

Many will argue that when you have a last name like 'Kardashian' and a husband such as Kanye West, you're already a celebrity. Therefore, becoming popular on social media and leveraging that popularity into revenue is a slam dunk, and consequently, it's not realistic to compare Kim Kardashian West to a consumer brand.

But Kim Kardashian West *is* a brand; so let's analyze some of her social media activity to look at what she does well, and which most companies *fail* to do at all.

First, Kim is a real person. A glance at her Twitter or Instagram accounts reveals Kim at home with her husband Kanye West and their kids. When was the last time that your CEO posted on social media what he or she does on the weekends when they are away from their office? There's something to be said about being human on social media. People gravitate to what feels relatable and 'real'.

Next, she interacts with her fans. Wow. Kim Kardashian West uses social media to engage with her fans, yet most companies struggle with replying to tweets and Instagram direct messages on the daily. If you want to grow your fanbase you need to make those that are paying attention feel valued in the hope that they'll advocate for you to their networks.

She is a savvy businesswoman who has found the perfect combination of showcasing her real, authentic-self on social media when the TV cameras aren't rolling – which makes her fans and community feel closer to her – along with shining a spotlight on her business endeavors and products. When she does try to sell products such as lipstick, she showcases real people such as herself or her family, while providing offers that are time-bound with a clear expiration date, which creates a sense of urgency and exclusivity. In one instance, she showcases her sister Kourtney using the product by way of a natively uploaded video on Twitter – similar to what you'd expect to see from a beauty influencer on YouTube – along with a link to buy in the text.

Kim Kardashian West is one example that brands can learn from to become more 'real' and relatable as business entities on social media. However, if you want to learn how to become a better storyteller, there's nobody better than Khaled Mohamed Khaled, otherwise known by his stage name 'DJ Khaled'.

If you've never heard of DJ Khaled before, hit 'pause' on reading right now, go to YouTube and type in 'DJ Khaled Snapchat' for historical context on what I'm about to explain because outside of Kim Kardashian West there's nobody else that receives more views on social media than DJ Khaled.

It's debatable whether or not Snapchat made DJ Khaled, or DJ Khaled made Snapchat but what is fact is that DJ Khaled seemingly went from being just another hip-hop DJ to an A-list media mogul, *New York Times* Best Selling Author and prominent brand spokesperson – all thanks to social media.

In 2015, Snapchat began to catch a 'buzz' as an alternative to Facebook. It was wildly popular among younger Millennials and college students who didn't want to post content that would stick around 'for ever' as is the case with Facebook. The entire premise of Snapchat was around 'storytelling' meaning unlike Facebook and Twitter, which had a newsfeed where you could post text-based content, Snapchat content came in the form of a static image, which would only appear on an end user's phone screen for a few seconds, or a video, which would run for as long as 10 seconds at a time. Think of Snapchat as 'Twitter meets YouTube'. Content is visual, short and intended to keep users coming back regularly for more.

One evening in December 2015, DJ Khaled went for a jet ski ride and ended up stranded at sea, which he documented on Snapchat thus sending social media into a frenzy and creating one of the first viral moments ever on Snapchat.

From that December day forward, the legend of DJ Khaled was born. Seemingly overnight the internet couldn't stop talking about DJ Khaled. From magazine covers to internet memes, he was everywhere. In the days, weeks and months following his meteoric rise, DJ Khaled began seeing 3–4 million views per Snap (Runcie, 2017). In the process, DJ Khaled taught us about daily storytelling and a new language – of marketing.

From 'major key alert' to 'they don't want you to win' to 'bless up', DJ Khaled's sayings became pervasive pop culture phrases. His phrases became a new level of 'cool', whether you were black, white, Hispanic, old, young or in-between, to use in social media content. Despite not following many celebrities on social media, I became hooked on watching DJ Khaled on social media every day. I couldn't get enough. Soon, corporate brands began to take notice, and DJ Khaled's social media popularity became mainstream.

Silk, a plant-based milk brand, hired DJ Khaled for a traditional TV commercial using his own Snapchat content. Fundamentally, DJ Khaled, who isn't the best looking or most eloquently spoken character, was influencing us on how to make healthier choices in our lives.

In 2018, Weight Watchers named DJ Khaled a brand ambassador, which increased their stock price by 8 per cent in one day. Then, you have brands like Palmer's Cocoa Butter, which signed DJ Khaled to an endorsement deal to teach us how to nourish our skin, followed by Turbo Tax who rode DJ Khaled's tagline of 'rise up, bless up' and popularity to turn Khaled into a spokesperson for doing your taxes. Let's not forget about what to drink after you do your taxes – apple-flavored Ciroc vodka.

The rise of DJ Khaled isn't science by any stretch of the imagination, but there is a science to growing one's popularity online.

There's a reason why K-Swiss hired Gary Vaynerchuk to be a spokesperson with his signature shoe. There's a reason why Samsung enlisted YouTuber Casey Neistat to be a spokesperson for their company. It's the same reason why Diageo and Intuit signed DJ Khaled and why Nike signed basketballer LeBron James – they get your attention.

People like to see celebrities acting like normal people 'and that's what people want with their creators', said Greg Galant, CEO and Co-Founder of Sawhorse Media, in a recent episode of *Real Talk*. 'What you get through social media now, especially in the story format through Snapchat and Instagram, is much more candid than you've ever had before and in fact that's what makes it work.'

As consumers, we get tired of seeing and hearing the same marketing rhetoric from brands. However, when someone – whether a celebrity or an influencer or an everyday person – in your newsfeed connects with you on a personal level because they shop like you and do the things that you do, that's the magic in marketing. Paradoxically, we crave excitement and what feels 'new', yet at the same time we love everything about what feels familiar.

What DJ Khaled seemingly introduced us to through Snapchat – and similarly on Instagram Stories – was the craving for a continuous stream of content. Think about this. What happens at every company at 5 pm Monday through Friday? The employees at your favorite company go home. Therefore, they disappear on social media – like a Snapchat post, which is why every brand should be more like DJ Khaled and less like a brand.

Ultimately, where all of this area of marketing is headed is for your company to begin hiring employees as visual storytellers. It's unrealistic to assume that companies will have ungodly amounts of money in their marketing budget to hire influencers or even celebrities like DJ Khaled as company spokespeople. However, if you're already paying a marketing manager $65,000 per year to work for you, why not turn that person into the face of your company's Instagram channel? I'd be more compelled to follow a brand online where I know there will be a person speaking to me versus a logo. Who wants to hear from a logo? Nobody.

At the beginning of this chapter, I wrote 'influencer marketing doesn't work' because it doesn't, but the point that I want to drive home to you is around ambassadorship. You don't need influencers; you need ambassadors. These are the people who fit the profile of your target customer. There's a likelihood they are your target customer. An ambassador is someone who can connect with your social media audience in an authentic and relatable manner because they embody what your company does.

The difference between an 'influencer' and 'ambassador' are that an influencer is someone with perceived social media reach who is paid to promote your brand or product for a limited period, whereas an ambassador is someone who you pay for a set period to act as a company spokesperson. I would think differently about the business of influencer marketing – and so would your customers – if more brands hired creators as ambassadors because then it would feel authentic and less forced. What do you think?

Let's be honest, besides acting as a temporary band-aid for engagement, influencers are able to fill a void for brands – content.

Most brands struggle with creating content, especially storytelling, because if it's coming from a brand, it has to look and feel a certain way. Content that comes from a person feels natural even if they are overtly selling to you as we've seen from Kim Kardashian

West and DJ Khaled. This is why when you analyze what influencers bring to a brand it's not even their following that's valuable, but it's their persona. A marketable persona isn't something that every corporate marketer or small business owner inherently has; it's developed over time just like any other talent. Once again, this is why I predict companies will begin to hire individuals who are good storytellers.

In 2018, one of the most popular songs of the year was 'In My Feelings' by Drake. The music video to 'In My Feelings' has 187 million views and counting on YouTube. Meanwhile, the song was made additionally popular thanks to an Instagram post by a comedian who goes by the name of Shiggy, who made a video on Instagram of him dancing to the song that went viral and started the 'In My Feelings Challenge' sensation.

Like DJ Khaled's now infamous jet ski story on Snapchat, the #InMyFeelingsChallenge became a viral internet sensation which had everyone from celebrities to reality stars to 'everyday' people doing the dance challenge. To put it into perspective the popularity of the challenge, the original video on Instagram posted by Shiggy has over 7 million views to date whereas Walmart (which has 34 million Facebook fans and is one of the largest corporations in the world) received only a little over 200 engagements for one of its annual 'Black Friday Sale' posts on Facebook, even though Black Friday is one of the largest shopping days of the year for Walmart.

So do you want to be like Drake and Shiggy and have people speaking about you on social media or do you want to be like Walmart – a big brand that doesn't get the same reach and engagement?

It's no secret that celebrities and influencers today have discovered that the key to success is to engage fans; this not only leads to popularity but gets the fans to follow their recommendations.

Five key points for social media success

If your company is struggling with social media engagement, below are five key points to keep in mind for social media success:

1. Be real

Whether you're Nike, Coca-Cola or Walmart, today's consumer doesn't want to be sold to, they want to be engaged. The reason why influencer marketing exists and why people spend time consuming content from online personalities like Jake and Logan Paul, Tai Lopez and others is because these are real people who have a voice and thoughts to share with their fans. They're also entertaining. There's a story to follow. Consumers wake up in the morning excited to see what they might have missed from the night before, and they look forward with anticipation to seeing what's next in the sequence. Every brand is capable of doing this. It's not hard to replicate.

There's a large disparity online today between the world's biggest corporations and entertainers – ie, 'influencers'. Whereas it can take a company months, or even a year, to catch up and implement how they're going to be 'authentic', creators live it every day and give their communities what they want – an inside glimpse of who they are. All companies should look at what DJ Khaled does and model their employees to be their very own storytellers.

2. Be relevant

You don't have to be on every social network to be successful, but you should be on the ones where your customers are, and you should aim to tap into social networks where you can get the most reach and possible engagement. Having a presence on platforms like Twitter and Instagram, where content can be seen by non-followers by leveraging hashtags, mixed in with a content strategy that showcases your employees authentically and spotlights your goods, products and services through stories can go further than investing in say, Facebook Ads or highly produced videos. DJ Khaled has shown us how to tap into a highly active platform like Snapchat and now Instagram to take our followers behind the scenes through daily storytelling. The same tactics can be applied by virtually every company.

3. Don't sell

I know what you're thinking: 'I'm in business, how am I supposed to not sell?' But today's consumer is ignoring your sales rhetoric and instinctively swiping past your posts, which are perceived to be an offer versus a hook to engage. Companies today are struggling with using social media because they're focusing on the end-game (ie, the sale) versus the path to purchase, which involves creating brand awareness (being actively seen), tapping into conversations (otherwise known as engaging) with users, which builds loyalty, and acknowledging who their customers are.

While there's no easy way to monetize your online community, draw inspiration from DJ Khaled, who organically weaves Ciroc vodka into the narrative of his storytelling like you'd see product placement in a movie, or Kim Kardashian West, who will give you four or five Instagram posts about her family and friends – and then right-hook you with her business.

4. Celebrate success

The most significant competitive advantage that social media provides is the ability to listen to what's said about your brand, competition and industry. Whenever someone buys from your company and shares an online review, tweet or tags your brand, that's an opportunity for you to acknowledge your customer and celebrate the occasion. Where a lot of brands fail is that they're understaffed to the point where they completely ignore what's being said about their brand unless they're @mentioned and often engage only if it's a complaint or customer service-related post. Going forward, embrace and acknowledge the good just as you would the bad. An interaction is an opportunity to build customer loyalty further and repeat business.

5. Win more

DJ Khaled's most notable song 'All I Do is Win' can easily be the anthem for any entrepreneur or business owner who aspires to be at the top of her industry. However, how exactly do you 'win more'? Be consistent. What's helped DJ Khaled and Kim Kardashian West become two of the most recognized faces online isn't their looks or last names but instead being consistently in your face through your iPhone screen.

Social media isn't a 9 to 5 operation; it's open 24/7, year-round. Whether it's outsourcing community management or delegating your content marketing and storytelling strategies to employees, companies must realize that in the game of online marketing the brands who make the most noise combined with getting others to share their posts are the ones who will ultimately win the most. However, it begins with the first point of 'be real', which DJ Khaled and Kim Kardashian-West show us every single day.

Ten steps to telling the perfect story

Whether you're a B2B or B2C brand, you have the opportunity to be real with your customers and engage in genuine storytelling rather than just posting sales rhetoric. To become a better story-teller like DJ Khaled and other influencers, you can follow these 10 steps:

1. Define your objective

Think about why you want to share stories more specifically than to increase sales. Do you want to educate viewers about a problem your company solves? Do you have a great company culture that you want to share with others?

2. Eye on the prize

Stay focused on the three primary reasons why people use social: to be social, to be entertained and to be informed. Your brand can hit at least one of those three areas, no matter what industry you're in.

3. Create content relevant to the platform

Your audience might differ from network to network, or they might use certain platforms differently, such as LinkedIn for work and Snapchat for fun. As such, your storytelling should be relevant to what your audience wants to see on that platform.

4. Identify your storyteller(s)

Whether it's your CEO or your IT intern, start by looking within your organization to see if there's someone who enjoys sharing stories and can communicate your brand's narrative. In addition to employees, customers can be great storytellers for your brand, and social media gives you the opportunity to listen to and find them.

Taking what you learned in Chapter 3 'How to be savage AF – like Randy', harness the power of Twitter and Instagram search to see who is tweeting or posting about your brand and competition too. Finding advocates who already buy from you – or your competition – shouldn't be hard. The challenge is to turn them into product storytellers as 'ambassadors' for you.

For example, I am a fan and customer of Cole Haan. If you are on Instagram and run a search for #iwearcolehaan, you will see over 400 user-generated posts from customers. None of the posts in the thread have been replied to or acknowledged by Cole Haan. In this case, if I were Cole Haan's marketing team, I would go post-by-post and get to know who is posting content about my brand. When you take the time to do this exercise, you will find customers who have significant social media reach or at a minimum, the ones who take excellent photos. As I began to click through the images of Cole Haan shoes, one of the accounts that posted multiple product images is @KickSpotting, which has 75,000+ Instagram followers. Another picture was posted by @TheFiloDapper, a verified Instagram account with 69,000+ followers belonging to a men's fashion blogger. Sadly, these are real missed opportunities to leverage these advocates as brand ambassadors.

Once you've identified who is speaking about your brand, in this case let's assume you are a marketing manager for Cole Haan and you're going to engage @KickSpotting and @TheFiloDapper, the next step is to reach out to the account users directly and send them a message that reads like this:

> Hi AJ, we love the content that you posted about Cole Haan on your account @TheFiloDapper. Thank you for being a customer and a fan! Curious, would you be interested in becoming a brand ambassador for us and get a fresh new pair of shoes in the mail every month?

I realize that not every brand has a marketing budget to pay ambassadors or advocates; however, think about what your brand *can* offer as a form of payment. Let's assume that a new pair of Cole Haan shoes is $150, at 12 pairs a year that comes out to $1,800 worth of product for 12 Instagram posts coming from a men's fashion blogger with 69,000+ followers and now you have yourself a brand ambassador that's representing your brand without ever paying out cash. Compare that with what you might spend on social media advertising to get the same level of not only reach but genuine engagement and you'll often find that you come out ahead by paying ambassadors in some way. Just be sure you and your ambassadors properly disclose your relationships to stay in accordance with local laws and maintain consumer trust.

5. Storyboard your content

Good stories often require advance planning, so brainstorm with your internal marketing team, sales team, external media agency or whoever else you think can help you come up with clear, engaging storylines.

6. Keep content concise

Even if you have a great story to tell, it's difficult to keep your audience's attention given the vast amounts of competition for their time. So don't create an uphill battle for yourself by creating long-form content from the get go. At least in the beginning of your work toward building an engaged audience, keep content concise, such as limiting Instagram Stories or Snapchat Stories from around 30 seconds to 1 minute.

7. Create excitement on other social media channels

While you don't want to cross-post content without adjusting it for each platform, you can create cross-channel buzz by letting audiences on one platform, such as Twitter, know what you're doing on another platform, such as YouTube. As long as you natively post on each platform, your audience might be willing to follow you from one network to the next.

8. Ask your community to share

If you create engaging stories that you know your audience would actually be willing to share with their friends, go ahead and ask them to help spread the word. Doing so can help you exponentially expand your reach.

9. Don't go for the sale right away

Remember, hardly anyone goes on social media to see what brands are selling. Be social first and foremost, and then wait until the very end of a post to gently nudge people toward a sale. Otherwise, if you go for the quick sale, you'll increase the chances that your audience will drop off before the content ends.

10. Wait for the end for the call to action

Just as you should wait until the end of a post to go for the sale, you should also wait for the end for other calls to action, such as inviting your audience to follow you on another social media network or to attend an upcoming event.

Following these storytelling tips can help you seem more like DJ Khaled and Kim Kardashian West and less like an unrelatable brand.

Fame is hardly the only factor in social media success. There are plenty of celebrities who don't have much of a social media following, let alone an engaged one, because they're not being genuinely social and engaging in storytelling. For example, DJ Khaled wasn't always as famous as he is now, but he built up his brand through simple acts like showing what he's eating for breakfast and letting people see how he hangs out with his family. He lets people get an understanding of who he is both on and off the clock and you can do the same for your company.

For example, if you're on social media to market accounting software, don't expect to get much traction if you only post about the features your technology provides. Instead, share stories about how you met up with a client for a great dinner, or how you celebrated an employee's birthday in the office. Those are stories people can relate to.

However, your content can also be serious if that's a better fit for your brand. Many people are on social media to learn about new topics and improve their lives in some way, so you could share stories on how you prepare for meetings or your CEO's morning routine. As long as you are real and communicate how individuals do rather than slipping into sales-speak, you'll improve your chances of engaging your audience and forming real connections on social media. Those connections can then lead to customers intrinsically seeking out your products and services, as well as evangelizing your message to their own networks.

At your own brand, you may not have someone like a Kardashian or DJ Khaled to share stories, but you and your colleagues are real people that others should be able to relate to. Use this power to your advantage and share stories that bring your brand to life.

In the next chapter, you will learn how to transform your employees into advocates as the new faces of marketing for your brand.

Reference

Runcie, D (2017) Snap's IPO made its employees millionaires – why not DJ Khaled? *Wired*, 8 February [Online] https://www.wired.com/2017/03/snap-ipo-dj-khaled/ (archived at https://perma.cc/3C2X-K3R3) [accessed 24 April 2019]

08

Transforming your advocates into the faces of your brand

By this point you have read seven chapters of *The End of Marketing*, and hopefully you've warmed up to the notion that marketing (as we know it) is dead. This chapter that you're about to read is crucial because by the end you will have a valuable playbook that will help transform your employees and customer advocates into the new faces of marketing for your company.

To remain competitive and stand out in the noisy digital ocean that is social media you must prioritize humanizing your brand content, which means placing a human face and voice on your digital marketing channels and relying less on your brand's logo. While this theory is hard for most brand executives to accept because historically, we (the consumers) have associated iconic brand logos such as the Nike checkmark and Starbucks mermaid as faces of their brands. In the digital world, these logos alone don't carry the same weight for marketing as when you see a Starbucks or Nike store in your local shopping mall. Going forward, global brands like Nike, Starbucks, Coca-Cola and others will need to embrace this shift to remain digitally relevant to the masses. We are all consumers, and the last thing that we want in our social media newsfeed is to see another advertisement or salesy post coming from a brand – unless that advertisement includes such good story-telling that it moves us to share with our audiences because the ad itself *is* a movement.

For example, in 2018, amidst a lot of discussion and disagreement on social justice in the United States, Nike made a bold decision to create an advertising campaign focusing on equality. The ad featured the famed 'Just Do It' slogan and former NFL Quarterback Colin Kaepernick, who sparked a lot of the recent social justice discussions by starting a peaceful protest against unequal treatment of minorities by kneeling during the national anthem in 2016. The ad produced by Nike was tweeted out by Kaepernick and has gained over 11 million views along with 250,000+ retweets and over 556,000 'likes'. Nike struck gold by featuring Kaepernick to the tune of seeing an increase of $6 billion in market value as the company's stock grew following the announcement of this ad (Gibson, 2018).

Another brand that struck digital gold in recent memory was Budweiser, by sharing a tribute video to NBA star and likely future Hall of Famer Dwyane Wade of the Miami Heat. In Budweiser's ad, they feature five different stories of the impact that Dwyane Wade has made on individuals' lives including his mother. The advertisement in itself will make most people cry – as it did me. Moreover, the advertisement instantly became a topic of conversation across social media to the tune of 19 million+ video views combined with 73,000+ retweets and 193,000+ 'likes'. Obviously, the big question around these ads is: 'do they get people to buy?' However, the real takeaway is they do a phenomenal job at getting people to talk about the brand. Therefore, a significant brand awareness increase occurs for that moment in time, and that often organically leads to more sales.

These two examples showcase the impact that storytelling can have on a global brand such as Nike or Budweiser when you make people the face of your company. However, although every company is far from having the budgets that Nike or Budweiser have to produce these types of advertising campaigns or gain access to celebrities like Colin Kaepernick and Dwyane Wade – every company has the same opportunity to be human.

We are entering an era where the biggest companies in the world will need to humanize their brand content to remain digitally relevant; otherwise, they will cease to exist on our newsfeeds in the not so distant future. For example, Rebecca Minkoff is the co-founder of her eponymous fashion brand, and she's very active on social media as the face of her brand.

When executives build a personal brand on social media it can be valuable for the company overall. Customers want to connect with more than just a product, explained Minkoff on a recent episode of *Real Talk*. 'She wants to see me on a plane flying as a hot mess with my kids, or she wants to see what outfits I'm putting together or what I'm packing to go on a trip. So, it's about really continuing the dialogue, and if I can't meet you in person you feel like you know me and I'm your friend, and hopefully you want to wear your friend's stuff.'

Putting a face to a brand and forming a genuine connection with customers also helps companies become platform-agnostic. Minkoff's brand has always been active in engaging customers directly, from the early days of blogs, forums and MySpace to platforms like Instagram today. 'For us it was always about [whatever the new platform is], it allows us to talk to our customer, she appreciates that we're talking directly to her, we're surveying her, we're asking her questions for feedback and there's a two-way dialogue.'

Eventually, more big brands with recognizable logos will have specific people who become known as the digital faces of the brands, such as having a social media coordinator or a CMO become a well-known person to fans online. Content will range from short stories to longer-form original content (ie, a podcast, YouTube series, etc). It's going to happen.

There will also be a point in time where social networks like Facebook, Instagram and YouTube will begin to develop in-house talent – similar to how a movie studio casts roles for a film – and create content for brands that has all the look and feel of authentic, original content posted by a creator or influencer. As it stands now, the social networks aren't getting paid a percentage of every brand deal that an influencer secures for themselves. That will eventually come to an end, and the social networks will realize they are allowing their users to make thousands of dollars per post on their platforms without them (the social networks) making a dime from it. When you stop and think about it, the social networks themselves have infinite power to essentially 'turn on' more visibility to specific posts versus others. They can also cast for set roles knowing that for a creator to become an influencer in the eyes of a brand, all they need to do is find individuals – regardless of age or demographic – who can tell stories on camera, even an iPhone, and the social network handles the rest.

We are also at an intersection where marketers need to reevaluate the value that every social network provides to their organization and determine whether they should 'go dark' and retire a platform versus keeping it turned on for the sake of being there. It's already happening. Cosmetics company Lush took to social media to inform their 200,000+ Twitter followers that they would be closing down some of their UK brand social network accounts (though retail social accounts in the UK and brand accounts globally remain open) and reallocating resources elsewhere – openly calling out the fact that social networks like Twitter (and Facebook) are making it more difficult to reach fans and followers they've built up over the years. Furthermore, in the tweet by @LushLtd they stated 'we do not want to pay to appear in your newsfeed' calling out the obvious fact that it's pay-to-play if you aspire to have even a small percentage of your community see your content.

When you analyze the state of social media today and realize that the social networks themselves have infinite control through the algorithms to determine what is viewed versus what isn't – it's clear we're at the mercy of the social networks. They hold the keys to the kingdom; they own the cards to the deck. They are the house, and you must play by the house rules if you stand a chance at winning the game.

Your most significant competitive advantage isn't your logo or financial resources; it's your employees.

For every executive that claims customers are their brand's greatest asset, I call 'BS'. Without your employees, you don't have a brand. Employees of an organization are as critical for operational functions as they are for brand storytelling and communications. Today, an employee is much more than a person who stands at a cash register or sits in a cubicle; they are the face and voice of your brand – whether you choose to accept it or not. The thought of employees being the faces and voice of your brand can be a scary one. A lot can go wrong. With a smartphone and social media account, employees have the power to speak on behalf of your company and sway public perception if you don't have systems in place to help them effectively represent you.

For example, with Walmart, a quick Instagram search for #WalmartEmployee reveals over 3,200 posts to date. The majority of these Instagram posts represent employees headed to work and showing their love for the company they work for, or they involve some humor. What's interesting, and the key takeaway here, is that there are thousands of pieces of user-generated content on Instagram and Walmart doesn't appear to be in control of what is said about their brand.

So how do you control what employees post about you on social media? For beginners, you can't. However, my theory is to give your employees 'tools not rules'. Meaning if you give your employees the right set of resources for them to accurately represent your brand (ie, a platform with pre-written post content, guidelines on how to get the most out of social media as an ambassador, etc) and incentivize them accordingly, they're set up for success. What you don't want is for an employee to go rogue on social media and post whatever they want and whenever they want without any guidelines in place.

In the case of Starbucks, from rants and pet peeves to 'What to expect in Starbucks training' videos, which are publicly accessible on YouTube, Starbucks baristas are particularly passionate about their jobs at the famous brand. There's an entire BuzzFeed article titled '25 things Starbucks employees will never tell you' (Stopera and Stopera, 2019), which features a collection of tweets from Starbucks employees with #ProTips and #LifeHacks about improving your Starbucks experience, and Starbucks as a brand also jumped into the mix.

However, there will always be an employee that goes rogue. For example, in 2017 Starbucks decided it would introduce the world to the now infamous Unicorn Frappuccino, a drink that was sugary and full of calories but looked absolutely beautiful as content on Instagram. According to various reports, a week before the launch of the Unicorn Frappuccino, Starbucks employees took to sites such as Reddit to leak the new product and also vent about the time it takes to make, in addition to its foul taste. One of those employees was Brandon Burson of Colorado who on 19 April 2017 tweeted one of the most epic videos ever recorded by a disgruntled employee. He said: 'Today, it came out, and I have to tell you, *please don't get it*. I have never been so stressed out in my entire life, it has been insane! I have unicorn crap all in my hair and on my nose. If you love us, as baristas, *don't order it!*' Although Burson's tweet was deleted, the video of the outburst was picked up by news outlets around the world in addition to being turned into internet memes. A YouTube video from *Inside Edition* of Burson's rant has been seen 11 million+ times.

Employees also make an impact on how customers talk about brands on social media. A quick search for 'Starbucks barista' on Twitter reveals a real-time feed updated regularly throughout each hour of the day, as consumers of the brand tweet about their experience at their local Starbucks store. In some cases, their local baristas are community celebrities. Thus, companies need to embrace their employees as faces of their brands, and they need to effectively train their employees to adopt this mindset as well.

Why does employee advocacy really matter?

As described in the examples mentioned above, your employees are already active on social media and speaking about your brand without you monitoring it. With a strategy and technology in place, you can have more control over what's said publicly and, in most cases, activate your workforce to be an extension of your marketing team. Imagine for a moment that you work for a company that has thousands of employees, yet the dedicated social media arm is a small team of one or just a handful of employees who work in the marketing department. Running social media for your company can be daunting when you don't have a lot of resources (ie, people and money) to do cool 'stuff' like more prominent brands such as Nike and Starbucks. By activating your workforce of employees, you can have:

- A way to expand your brand reach beyond a few social media accounts to potentially thousands more, thus helping you drive more brand awareness and grow digital share of voice, which are two primary KPIs for most marketers.

- A direct impact on sales, as the more links that surface on social media that point back to your company website – from employees posting on social media – the more website visits you'll earn, potentially resulting in increased lead generation and sales opportunities.

- Additional brand trust: whether you're a B2B or B2C brand, people trust other people more than they do brands.

- Improved employee retention and a way to attract top talent: Having an employee advocacy strategy empowers your employees to have a voice as company ambassadors, which helps employees feel proud of working at your organization and gives them an opportunity to grow their own personal brands and careers.

Getting buy-in throughout the company

As I have learned first-hand throughout the years of working at brands and rolling out employee advocacy programs, and now as an agency owner doing it for clients, the question will come up from employees and executives: 'why does this matter?'

You must create the why *and* sell the value throughout your organization.

When working with financial services giant Western Union on rolling out their employee advocacy program, the first step was to convince leadership that activating thousands of global employees for the company would help to drive organic brand awareness through social media, followed by promoting positive brand perception and increasing the digital share of voice (SOV). By providing Western Union employees with a hub where they could access and share pre-approved social media content, Western Union would be able to control what employees were saying about a brand that's highly regulated and publicly traded, thus limiting risk and exposure. Whenever you're selling your business case to an executive leader it's critical that you state the value for the organization up front.

The next step was to show leadership that employees were already engaging organically without direction coming from corporate, with local events and sponsorships being of importance to employees. For most enterprise companies like Western Union, it's easy to see if your employees are speaking about you by running a quick search on Twitter for 'Your Company Employee' (for example, 'Western Union Employee') or by going to Instagram and running a hashtag search for #YourCompanyEmployee (for example, #WalmartEmployee).

As you build out your employee advocacy strategy, including your communication plan to introduce it to executives, the most critical part is 'Key Stakeholder Benefits', ie, how does it benefit your organizational silos? At Western Union, for instance, there are specific departments (eg, marketing, talent acquisition/HR, executive leadership, regional marketing and PR/communications) who view the benefits of social media and having employees as ambassadors differently. Therefore, it is up to you to develop a strategy for each group and meet with each organizational silo leader separately to get buy-in, such as by explaining to HR how employee advocacy can be used as part of a talent attraction and retention strategy.

As I have learned through experience, any time that you tell a person who works in a department outside of marketing that you are going to offer them an outlet for employees of the organization to promote their specific function they'll jump all over the opportunity. However, this can create more work for you and your team if you don't assign a group leader who will ultimately be responsible for providing you with content for each organizational silo. For example, if you're going to leverage employee advocacy to promote job openings at your company, it's up to one team member in HR to provide you with information and content which will go into a portal or platform for company-wide broadcasting.

Another example of effective employee advocacy programs comes from my time working at BMC Software in 2015. At the time BMC, which had 6,000 employees globally, had a social media presence that was established by the previous head of social media; however, there wasn't an employee advocacy strategy in place to activate its workforce of sales executives and developers into advocates. In search of a 'quick win' within my first 30 days on the job, I did two things: reduce the number of company-branded social media accounts from 100+ to only 12 and spearheaded the launch of BMC's employee advocacy program, which we called 'BeSocial'. This helped streamline our social media efforts and get everyone moving in the same direction so that we could build a more engaged following.

Before rolling out a legitimate employee advocacy portal, BMC corporate communications would regularly send out a company-wide email to motivate employees to share content across social media. I call this the 'old school method'.

If you currently don't have a go-to hub or technology platform, sending emails with recommend posts is one way to try to engage your employees. However, you may want to consider investing in a platform where all of your employees have access to login and post content. An employee advocacy platform will help streamline the process and increase user adoption. Brand messages reach 561 per cent further when shared by employees than when the same messages are shared via official brand social channels (Parry, 2017).

Four examples of employee advocacy tools to consider are:

- Elevate by LinkedIn
- Dynamic Signal
- Sprinklr
- Bambu by Sprout Social

While cost is essential when sourcing a vendor or technology service provider, you will want to go with a solution that's *easy* for your employees to sign up to and *easy* for your employees to see content to share. The primary factor in gaining mass user-adoption is simplicity, so look for a platform that you think your employees will easily pick up. The more steps and rules that you put in place the harder it will be to keep your employees engaged and committed. Secondly, keep your employees coming back to the platform by keeping your content fresh.

At BMC Software, I was fortunate to have executive support from my Chief Marketing Officer Nick Utton, who was in favor of activating our employees as advocates. Within weeks of starting with the company, we launched 'BeSocial' on the Sprinklr platform as an all-inclusive resource for BMC Software employees around the world to access corporate news and announcements as well as share social media posts already pre-written for Twitter, Facebook and LinkedIn, on topics ranging from industry events where BMC Software had a presence to unique, business-specific content.

Keys to successful employee advocacy program rollouts

The first step to a successful rollout is to beta test the platform that you select. Before beta testing with a small group of associates, you will want to ensure that there's a significant amount of content in the platform itself. At BMC, the home page of the platform had a header that said 'Boost Your Brand And BMC's' which set the stage for what employees could expect (the 'why') followed by seeing a three-step process describing how to sign up and what to do after login.

Our 'BeSocial' campaign offered employees the ease of signing up for the platform with their LinkedIn account. Whenever selecting a technology platform (eg, Elevate by LinkedIn, Bambu by Sprout, etc) be sure to go with an option that allows for single sign-on (SSO) using a company email address or the ability to sign up with an associate's social media account.

The next step is to have each participating associate login to a platform where content is categorized by company business unit or function (eg, careers/human resources, events, public relations/news, etc).

A benefit of having a streamlined employee advocacy strategy and content hub is that employees have a go-to resource to find content that's already written for them. In the example of 'BeSocial', employees connect their Twitter, Facebook or LinkedIn account and are able to immediately post content that's written for them in the form of a native post – including relevant hashtags – or posts can be scheduled similar to using Buffer or Hootsuite.

Within weeks of launching 'BeSocial', we had over 1,000 global employees registered, which resulted in thousands of new earned media impressions including website clicks. However, maintaining momentum after an initial rollout is critical. As the Global Head of Social Media, I made it a priority to get in front of as many teams throughout the business as possible. From human resources and talent acquisition to sales, it's a must-have to gain visibility for your program to secure adoption. Throughout my employment, I found myself presenting on weekly meeting conference calls to quarterly in-person sales training about the value that social media brought to the organization. The question of 'why is this important?' was a constant hurdle to overcome. In simple terms, the answer to 'why?' is this:

> More social media post shares by employees lead to more digital impressions and website visits, which ultimately results in more revenue and profit for companies.

How to keep up momentum after launching

Once you get buy-in, it's critical to assign a team leader for each business unit throughout your organization to contribute content every week, otherwise you and your marketing team will find yourself spending the majority of your week finding and writing content for your platform.

To recap, here's a helpful checklist to follow as you introduce employee advocacy at your organization:

- Meet with your executive leadership team, including key stakeholders, to sell them on the potential benefits of activating your company employees as brand advocates on social media.

- Select a technology provider that will serve as your all-inclusive 'content hub' whereby employees will login and have access to social media content.

- Survey your employees through your company intranet or internal communications to see who is passionate about promoting your company on social media. Also, leverage these surveys to discover who from your employee base is a natural storyteller or open to taking over your company social accounts.

- Before launching enterprise-wide, select a group of test users to pilot or trial a platform, and get feedback from your Beta group on what they like and don't like about the platform.

- Align with corporate communications to write an announcement from either your CEO or CMO about the program and why it's crucial to the company. For example, at BMC Software, my Chief Marketing Officer Nick Utton delivered an announcement via email to all employees on the day that we launched 'BeSocial' to drive excitement and awareness of the program.

- Create an FAQ document that lives on your company intranet or portal and serves as a training guide, as questions are sure to arise. Also, consider delivering a company-wide webinar on the benefits of personal branding to serve as live training for your employee advocacy program.

- Align with HR to ensure that all new employees are encouraged to sign up on their first day of employment, so you can ensure that you will always have a flow of new registrants.

- Last, report results and KPIs regularly to leadership as well as to your internal stakeholders to keep the momentum going strong. The KPIs that you will want to report on are: net new impressions, website clicks, leads and closed sales as a result of employee sharing. Within your platform, you can add website links that contain a tracking code to measure performance through a platform such as Google Analytics.

Figure 8.1   Example of content created by Shaun Ayala on Snapchat

SOURCE Shaun Ayala

Converting your employees into advocates doesn't only mean that you have them share content that you vet and authorize. It's also turning your employees into storytellers.

Meet Shaun Ayala, an award-winning Snapchat storyteller and artist. Shaun also happens to be on the marketing team at Best Buy yet he's world-renowned for the work that he does on Snapchat as his 'side hustle'. I've come to know Shaun personally over the last few years and am amazed by his artistic ability. I hired him as an influencer for my client DocuSign for one of their annual conferences, where he took over their Snapchat account.

By meeting Shaun and other talented creators, I realized that the vital differentiator that these influencers possess, which the average corporate marketer does not, is the ability to tell stories creatively, using the tools available – drawing, text, tags, sound, filters, GIFs – to captivate a stranger's attention through Snapchat or Instagram

Figure 8.2   Example of content created by Shaun Ayala on Snapchat

Figure 8.3   Example of content created by Shaun Ayala on Snapchat

SOURCE Shaun Ayala

Stories. During a conference years ago in Phoenix, Arizona, I distinctly remember telling Shaun that companies like Best Buy and others would eventually need to hire creatives – not marketers – to do the same work as him, but as employees. Most brands do not have the marketing budget to hire an influencer regularly, but they can start switching up the requirements of a social media marketer. And they will.

> Marketing *is* product storytelling and social media *is* the gateway.

Going forward, brands will need to hire employees who have social media storytelling skills the same way they will employ more in-house copywriters to produce captions to go along with eye-catching creative content produced in-house. Also, brands will need to hire dedicated analysts who can accurately decipher social media data and run optimized Facebook Ad campaigns.

At BMC Software, we were one of the first B2B companies to use Snapchat as a storytelling medium to tell our brand story. At a bare minimum, storytelling helps humanize your brand by putting a real face and voice in front of your social media community. Through Snapchat, we used storytelling to spotlight new employees, executives and various team members who would take over our account and do 'a day in the life' content.

We would also cross-promote our Snapcode on our Twitter account to drive new followers to BMC Software on Snapchat whenever we had an employee take over the account or would share content from a special occasion such as an industry conference.

As I shared in the last chapter, we all have access to the same tools as Kim Kardashian West and DJ Khaled. It's up to you to use them and incorporate the blueprint that works for high-profile celebrities into your company's strategy. If you don't use the tools, your competition likely will.

Begin by identifying potential storytelling opportunities, which include new hire orientation, a day in the life of possibilities, industry events and conferences, and product demonstrations. You should look to designate one day out of the week for an employee to take over your Snapchat or Instagram account as a tactic to show that your company is a fun place to work and showcase the work they are doing. This augments your content to feel like it's less about sales and more about creating human connections. Then, create content for Facebook, Twitter and LinkedIn to drive awareness of the takeover.

Remember, part of selling is to be real and relatable. The other half is addressing a need with a solution. Going back to Starbucks, imagine if, when the Unicorn Frappuccino came out, they had offered all 200,000+ employees globally a platform like 'BeSocial' for streamlined employee sharing, and then had select baristas take over their social media channels to 'show and tell' the making of the new product. If employees felt like they had more of a voice and ownership of the new product rollout, they might have felt less stressed and frustrated by the additional work it created.

For a company like Nike, aside from featuring high-profile celebrities in ads like the Colin Kaepernick example, they could take to Twitter and run a search to see who their most engaged fans are and enlist them to create customer takeover content for their brand channels. I'd imagine if you follow this approach within your brand, you will find customers who already buy from you that would be thrilled to participate in a takeover of your channels. Better yet, if you're struggling to produce video or blog content, ask your engaged fans and customers to send in a video to your company email of how they use your product. With their permission, you might be able to use this as native content on your Facebook page or when writing a blog post for republishing on your company website. Have fun with it too – you never know when you might spark the next viral challenge!

The advantage that you and your business will have by creating stories goes back to humanization. When you put a human face and voice on content, end users know who they are engaging with online. For the longest time, corporate brands and businesses have hidden behind the curtain, and that curtain is now being torn down because consumers crave transparency.

The ideas and tools outlined in this chapter are relevant for anyone that wishes to take their brand or company forward into the next wave of what's next for social media – the human economy. This is an era where being able to transform people into the faces of your brand effectively will define the future state of your company. The topic of turning employees into advocates is something that I've put into practice multiple times throughout my career. Whenever I think about 'the end of marketing' – and what's next – I think of a digital ecosystem where people are the faces of brands, not logos. I believe that companies will be forced to redefine what it means to be a 'marketer' and begin hiring those who have a skill set to tell stories. The art of 'storytelling' with a human face and voice has more value for an organization than an advertisement designed on a computer. I also think about the digital judgment day – AI versus humans – which you will learn more about in Chapter 9.

References

Gibson, K (2018) Colin Kaepernick is Nike's $6 billion man, *CBS News*, 21 September [Online] https://www.cbsnews.com/news/colin-kaepernick-nike-6-billion-man/ (archived at https://perma.cc/MMT6-7AJM) [accessed 24 April 2019]

Parry, S (2017) Employee advocacy – the modern day BBQ sell? [Blog] MSL Group, 19 April [Online] https://www.mslgroup.co.uk/latest/2017/employee-advocacy-the-modern-day-bbq-sell/ (archived at https://perma.cc/6BPC-7YA6) [accessed 24 April 2019]

Stopera, D and Stopera M (2019) 25 things Starbucks employees will never tell you, *Buzzfeed*, 11 April [Online] https://www.buzzfeed.com/mjs538/starbucks-tips (archived at https://perma.cc/LR7K-EGHS) [accessed 29 April 2019]

09
Judgment day
The battle of AI versus humans

Over the last two chapters, you've been taught the playbook for storytelling like a celebrity, with examples from Kim Kardashian West and DJ Khaled, to transform your brand into one that people want to follow and tell their friends about, instead of being just another company on the internet that's pushing their latest sale. You've also learned about leveraging your organization's most significant asset – its employees and customers – into engaged brand advocates and storytellers to amplify your reach beyond your company's social media accounts. Now, to connect the dots, you're about to learn why everything you've learned up to this point is not an option but a requirement to stay digitally relevant and employed. The reason I am passionate about humanizing brand marketing through people and not logos, and what has led me to write this book, is that the humanization of marketing is our last line of defense before technology replaces thousands of marketing jobs – including the role of social media managers – with bots.

My theory about the future of marketing leads me to an ecosystem in which machine learning, predictive analytics and artificial intelligence (AI) will reign supreme. There will come a day when the role of a social media manager or community manager at a brand is replaced altogether by these forms of technologies. Therefore, in the same manner that corporations need to hire in-house creators to grow an internal roster of brand storytellers, they will also need to retain data analysts who will be tasked with programming armies of bots for specialized tasks and functions currently done by humans, such as customer service and sales.

Growing up in the 1990s one of my favorite movies was *Terminator 2: Judgment Day*. In the film, Arnold Schwarzenegger's character is sent forward in time to protect human civilization from a mutiny in which robots rule the Earth. Inspired by *Terminator* the movie, this chapter should wake you up to realize that we have already entered an era of AI versus human – and there's no turning back.

To put this into context, begin by understanding the purpose of the following technologies, which are already being leveraged by the world's largest corporations:

Machine learning

Machine learning is a branch of artificial intelligence based on the idea that systems can learn from data, identify patterns and make decisions with minimal human intervention.

Meaning, through machine learning, Google can know who you are as a person, what you do for fun, where you go shopping and what your interests are, based on years of you running searches. The data that Google collects on you helps them segment you into categories, which can then be leveraged by advertisers. This is why whenever you run ads on Google's platforms (including YouTube) you can target users based on various interests and demographics. As a fun fact, Google processes over 40,000 search queries every second on average (Internet Live Stats, 2019).

Predictive analytics

Predictive analytics is used to make predictions about unknown future events and uses techniques from data mining, statistics, machine learning and artificial intelligence to analyze current data to make predictions.

In the case of e-commerce and retail, Amazon has data on what its customers are buying and how often to leverage predictive analytics modelling, for example, to anticipate when customers are ready to place their next order of Tide PODS and then also recommend ancillary goods for purchase, by leveraging historical data of other customers who share similar buying patterns.

Artificial intelligence

Artificial intelligence, otherwise known as 'AI', is the ability of a computer program or machine to think, learn and perform tasks that normally require a human operator. AI is also a field of study that tries to make computers 'smart', and as machines become 'smarter', they become increasingly capable of performing tasks once thought to require human intelligence.

The future is happening now

To put my theory into perspective, imagine a world in which all of the data that lives on the internet, including company CRM systems, allows brands to develop a 'social bot' to cut through the digital noise and go directly to customers right before they're set to purchase without having to send a single tweet or direct message – from a human.

A social media bot such as this can be either an application or profile on a social media platform that is automatically programed to generate messages, follow accounts, reply to or share particular hashtags, usually using machine learning.

Corporations, which are always under pressure to keep overhead costs to a minimum and have smaller social media teams, are already programming Facebook page bots through ManyChat and Chatfuel to perform tasks, such as community management, which they would have historically paid a human to complete as their primary job function.

So, what happens when Twitter opens up its API to these programs and your company no longer needs to hire a team of community managers to manage the volume of inbound @mentions? Or, better yet, what happens when AI can crawl through Twitter in real time and identify who's a potential customer for your brand? If right now I can order a pizza or flowers from a chatbot, what happens when predictive analytics and machine learning empower AI to take years' worth of tweets to automate copywriting? Imagine if all of your blog posts, tweets and Facebook content are automatically created using an AI that has enough data points to know what type of content will get the highest engagement or conversion and on what day. Eventually, a marketing team, in this doomsday scenario, would be a small unit of data analysts programming systems to run themselves to yield the highest monetary ROI. Meanwhile, thousands of marketing jobs will disappear for ever. Sadly, these are all likely scenarios, which we will see come to fruition before 2030.

From auto-liking content, auto-following accounts and auto-commenting, there's a lot that you can do right now with the assistance of a bot without investing thousands of dollars into building your bot platform or without relying on a human being to complete simple tasks that otherwise would take hours or days to manually complete – which is appealing at first glance.

Knowing first-hand how frugal corporations can be when it comes to hiring employees combined with the fact that businesses are in business to grow their revenue at the lowest cost per employee, it's not a matter of if but when the mantra of 'automate everything' will be implemented by businesses of all sizes. However, although automating menial tasks sounds enticing on the surface, it's really more like quick fix than an effective long-term strategy for growing your business.

Thanks to advances in technology there's a lot that you can automate in this new world of business but if there's one thing that you cannot automate it's a real, authentic relationship with another human being. Relationships are at the epicenter of all that we strive to do in business, and while there are cases for bots that make good business sense, there are also bad uses for bots.

A few years ago, I was invited to speak at a conference in Copenhagen, Denmark about 'the future of social media'. In researching at the time, I was fascinated by the point that mobile messaging apps would soon account for a far greater portion of mobile messaging activity compared to mobile carriers. What this means is that messaging apps such as Messenger and WhatsApp today have more people using their platforms for messaging others than that of wireless carriers.

We are no longer talking about only social media but rather apps that cross over between social media and utility (ie, the ability to message). This is what I refer to as the 'private media'. Whenever I get asked 'What's next for social media?' or 'What social network should I keep my eye on?' I always say that the most significant social network that already exists that nobody yet is openly talking about is Facebook Messenger.

Right now, with over 1 billion registered users, Facebook Messenger is the fourth largest social media network in existence only behind Facebook, YouTube and WhatsApp (which Facebook acquired in 2014). The reason why you shouldn't ignore Facebook Messenger is that it offers your brand more than just another platform to drive website traffic, it's a platform to drive revenue. Messenger is Facebook's version of WeChat, a Chinese multipurpose messaging, social media and mobile payment app developed by Tencent, which by 2018 was one of the world's largest standalone mobile apps by monthly active users, with over 1 billion monthly active users.

As I was preparing to speak in Copenhagen, I decided there was no better way to talk about the future of social media and bots than to use a 'real-life' bot and report on my experience. The first step was to go to the Discover tab within Messenger. Discover is where users can browse and find Messenger bots from businesses. Organized by categories such as News, Travel and Shopping, users can find thousands of bots within the Discover section of Messenger. In my case, I attempted to book a hotel room at Marriott strictly through the Marriott bot.

The first prompt on Marriott's bot was to select either 'Find a Hotel' or 'Customer Care'. I wrote 'Hi, I'm looking for a hotel in

Copenhagen. Can you help?' purposely to see if the AI would pick up on words instead of clicking on the prompt. No surprise, the word 'hotel' prompted the AI to reply with a generic response. I was given the options 'Find a hotel' or 'Customer care' again with the additional option of 'How Does This Work?'. I clicked on 'Find a Hotel' and was then asked where I was going, to which I proceeded to reply with 'Copenhagen'.

This is where it gets interesting. Apparently, the Marriott bot did not recognize that Copenhagen is the name of a city, so it asked me three times where I wanted to go until I replied with 'Denmark!!!' only to find out there were no available hotels in Demark. The bot then offered me the option to 'Start a New Search' or 'Customer Care,' to which I selected 'Customer Care'. The bot responded saying its customer care team was most responsive during certain hours (meaning not in real time for the moment in which I was using it) and asked me to type my question so someone could get back to me.

A few days later when I was already in Copenhagen and decided to stay at an Airbnb instead, I received a message from presumably a 'real person' on Marriott's social media team informing me that Marriott has two hotels in Copenhagen. Its bot didn't understand the message. Ironically, upon replying and informing Marriott that I was already in Copenhagen and had gone with Airbnb instead, the bot auto-replied, beginning the 'Find a Hotel' sequence once more.

As of right now, a bot cannot replace human interaction. However, it's subject to change as machine learning, and AI, become more advanced and can cross-check words typed by the end user with a company website in real time. As evidenced in the Marriott example, dialogue with a bot was limited to what is programed based on keywords and phrases.

I call this a 'bot fail'.

Continuing with my experimenting, leading up to the writing of this chapter I decided to try ordering a pizza from Domino's within Messenger. To be funny, I used the waving hand emoji to signal a 'hello'. Domino's bot didn't understand what a waving hand emoji sign means though. Our interaction went as follows:

Me: *wave emoji*

Domino's: I'm sorry, I seem to be having trouble understanding.

Me: Hello

Domino's: Hello! This is Dom, the Domino's ordering assistant bot. How can I help? New order. Reorder. Track order.

Me: New order

Domino's: Ok, what is your email address so we can send your order confirmation?

Me: *(provides email)*

Domino's: How do you want to pay for this order?

Me: Debit or Credit

Domino's: For your security, credit/debit card payments are taken through www.dominos.com. Once your order has been placed, I can still help you track it (Link to Complete Checkout provided).

Me: Order Complete

Domino's: (Confirms/provides delivery address + total)

Me: What now?

(Then I started to have some fun with the bot and test its capabilities.)

Domino's: You're welcome! Please tell me if there is anything else I can help you with.

Me: Why is Domino's pizza better than Pizza Hut?

Domino's: Sorry. I don't understand. How can I help?

Me: Pizza Hut, do you know them?

Domino's: Sorry. I don't understand. How can I help?

Me: What's your favorite topping?

Domino's: I'm sorry. I don't understand.

From hotel reservations to ordering a pizza from Domino's, Messenger bots have promise but feel like a clunky and cumbersome experience. As I experienced with Domino's, after giving all of my information including name, address, email and phone number, I was still prompted to visit their website to place my order, which defeats the purpose of using the bot and as a customer takes more time to complete. Even after placing my order on Domino's website I was prompted by the bot experience to check out once again.

To create a bot of your own, you will want to use ManyChat or Chatfuel. While building a Messenger chatbot isn't difficult and only takes a few minutes to set up unless you're making a robust chat experience, like Marriott or Domino's, creating an end-to-end chat sequence is where you will want to invest time carefully. In addition to offering back-end analytics such as subscriber counts, ManyChat and Chatfuel also allow you to send push notifications to your subscribers similar to how you would use an email service provider for email marketing.

As of now, it's debatable whether bots are more relevant to corporate or personal brands. Entrepreneur Grant Cardone has a bot that sends me a daily push notification with a single post from Grant. To be candid, I prefer this approach to Facebook marketing to posting content to a business page. Also, it's more effective from my perspective to have the ability to send a push notification to thousands of users on Messenger – similar to an email newsletter send – than to use a bot for customer service or e-commerce as evidenced by the Marriott and Domino's Pizza examples.

Now, before we get to the goodness of bots – let's address the not-so-good tactics for using social media bots:

Buying 'fake' followers and 'fake' engagement

It's not an uncommon practice for both influencers and 'wannabe influencers' to purchase bot accounts to follow them or engage with their content. If you've considered this tactic know that you're only kidding yourself and nobody else. Companies are specializing in 'bot farming': creating armies of bots, which are technically 'real' social media accounts, but an actual person doesn't actively operate them, therefore, the fake followers will only represent a number that has no value whatsoever.

Following and unfollowing tactics

If you want to avoid getting 'shadow banned' or temporarily blocked by a social network, do not play the game of following an account for the sake of them auto-following you, only for you to unfollow them.

Auto-like and auto-comment

For experimenting and research, I have used various engagement bots over the years. While auto-commenting 'Follow for follow?' and 'Like my post!' across thousands of Instagram posts may get you some followers they're not going to develop into quality followers if you aren't cultivating the relationship. This comes back to most of what you've learned up to this point in the book.

While I firmly believe that AI will effectively disrupt how we market and eliminate many marketing jobs in the not too distant future, saving time that would be applied doing transactional customer service while reallocating resources toward outbound engagement should be a key priority. You don't need to spend a lot of money to hire an outside agency to build you a bot. Instead, create an auto-reply Messenger bot, which will take you less than one minute to build.

The first step to building a Messenger chatbot within Facebook will be to go to your page settings within Facebook followed by 'Messaging' on the left side of the page followed by 'Response Assistant'.

Figure 9.1 How to build a messenger bot within Facebook

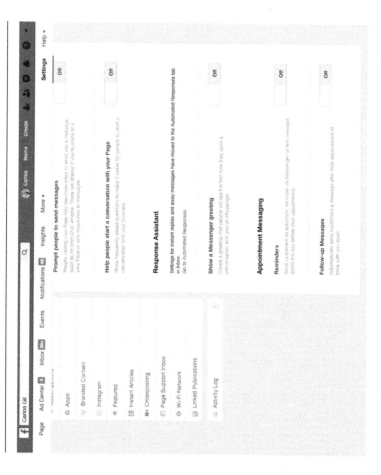

SOURCE Facebook via Carlos Gil

You will have the option to set an instant reply to anyone who messages your page. This could include a greeting and details of how soon you'll get back to them.

Figure 9.2   Example of 'Instant Reply' feature within Messenger bot

Although an instant reply won't provide you with the robust chat sequence experience that you can set up using ManyChat or Chatfuel, it's the first step to automating responses to customers who otherwise get overlooked during business hours including off-hours and weekends. It's also an excellent way to automatically let your customers know that you will reply to them within a set period (eg, 24 hours) or you can point them to your website FAQ section too. At a minimum, you can set up your chatbot to reply with a link to your latest YouTube video, an e-book for lead generation or a Facebook post that you'd like to drive added attention to, as seen below from my page.

Figure 9.3   Examples of Instant Reply responses using custom GIFs

SOURCE Facebook via Carlos Gil

There is value in AI and social media chatbots, so I pose the question that is probably on your mind now: 'How will this affect my job if I work in social media?'

Done effectively, AI and social media chatbots will free up time, which hopefully will allow you and your team to do what is required moving forward to elevate your brand presence. That is, storytelling and direct one-to-one engagement with your customers. As I've demonstrated throughout this book, there is one task that a bot cannot do yet and that is replacing a human face and voice. As I've stressed, humanizing your brand over the next decade will be your greatest competitive advantage.

In a digital ecosystem where every minute Snapchat users share 527,760 photos, more than 120 professionals join LinkedIn, users watch 4,146,600 YouTube videos, 456,000 tweets are sent on Twitter and Instagram users post 46,740 photos, information overload combined with automation will continue to make end users feel alienated and emotionally removed from what they perceive to be advertorial content coming from brands (Marr, 2019).

Once we get to the point where you can't determine if you are messaging with a chatbot or a human being, the human face and voice will be your last method of offense.

CASE STUDY Lil Miquela

Meet Instagram username @lilmiquela. On the surface, she appears to be just another 19-year-old Instagram influencer with 1.5 million followers.

Lil Miquela has content from attending Coachella, collaborations with A-list celebrities such as J Balvin, and even posts video content on Instagram Stories – yet, she's not a real person. She's a computer-generated cyborg, and the most mind-blowing fact of all is that you can't even tell because she looks 'real' and has video content with a voice.

Lil Miquela is just one example of what your company is competing against. As I wrote at the beginning of this chapter, the battle of AI versus human has already begun. Now, if you want to stand out in a world that's set to be dominated by AI, chatbots and computer-generated 'influencers' you should immediately begin storytelling and creating internal influencers through employee advocacy (as explained in Chapters 7 and 8). Specifically, when using messenger apps, keep the following best practice in mind:

Make it personal

Personalization and humanization go hand in hand. Whenever you personalize the experience, you can make a deeper human connection with your customer, and I'm not referring to only using their name in a direct message or tweet. What I am implying you should do to win over your customers is understand what's important to them by paying attention to what they're talking about, what are key dates in their life (ie, birthday, anniversary, etc) and engage them around interests that are relevant to them more than your brand. For example, I fly with American Airlines often enough that American Airlines' community manager should reach out and personally introduce him or herself. This is no different from what the manager at a restaurant does when they come around the dinner table to see how the server is performing. For a brand like American Airlines it might be difficult to reach everyone, but at least start in waves beginning with your most loyal customers and then working backward. By scrolling through my feeds on Twitter and Instagram, you can see that I travel often and get haircuts whenever I'm visiting a new city. American Airlines could use these publicly known details to shoot me a tweet or Instagram direct message informing me of a barbershop I should check out whenever I am in a specific town or make a few local suggestions on what to do. This is what I mean by making interactions personal. While it's a lot of work, it's going above and beyond to make a customer feel valued.

Message your customers with video or voice

As evidenced in the Marriott and Domino's examples, Messenger bots can help a brand grow its market share and revenue with valuable e-commerce tools built into the platform, yet it still falls short on providing the human element of engaging with a person. Both Messenger and Instagram allow you to send a voice message to users – I would suggest you immediately begin leveraging this as a tactic for your customers to hear directly from you (a real person) instead of leading them to believe that they might be interacting with a bot. Imagine how you can take customer service to the next level if you start using built-in features such as FaceTime calling and video messages for your customers to hear and see you. In a bot-driven world where you are competing with computer cyborgs like Lil Miquela, having your employees step from behind the digital curtain isn't a bad thing at all – it's a competitive advantage.

Make real people the faces of your campaigns

I was with a client recently who was showing me the creative for their latest advertising campaign and was stunned to see that the images they were using for everything from email marketing to social media posts featured stock images purchased from Shutterstock that appeared to be actual customers of the company. Why fake it when you can recruit your existing customers and paying advocates to be the faces of your next brand campaign? Better yet, crowdsource content and encourage your social media community, which includes employees, to actively post content with your brand @username posted for a chance to appear in an upcoming brand campaign.

The world of social media has enough people faking their way to fame and doing whatever it takes to gain five minutes of digital attention. Don't contribute to the noise by ignoring your greatest assets: your customers and employees. They can represent you in a manner in which no influencer or bot ever will; they're real and authentic to your brand.

In the next chapter we'll look at the power of persuasion – from writing post copy to building relationships, it's a critical element in everything you do online.

References

Internet Live Stats (2019) Google search statistics, 8 May [Online] https://www.internetlivestats.com/google-search-statistics/ (archived at https://perma.cc/3ZDF-CGNC) [accessed 8 May 2019]

Marr, B (2019) How much data do we create every day? The mind-blowing stats everyone should read [Online] https://www.bernard-marr.com/default.asp?contentID=1438 (archived at https://perma.cc/6BF3-U7DP) [accessed 8 May 2019]

10
The power of personality and persuasion

As I was writing this book, I thought to myself 'How can I weave the chapters together, so each gives way to the next?' The beginning of the book gave you a comprehensive purview of the world today as it pertains to marketing and advertising, followed by the theory that the way to compete in this new era of digital business is by humanizing your brand: by making people, including your employees, the new faces of your company. This chapter will put into context how exactly you can sell yourself (or the product/service you represent) and become a thought leader within your industry, but it will also teach you how to leverage the internet as a person, not a corporation, to build fruitful connections that may lead to business opportunities by tapping into your greatest 'superpower' – the power of you.

I am a believer in the power of personal branding because I am a by-product of what happens when you build relationships through social media. I wouldn't have the career that I have today or be writing this book had I not lost my job in the financial services industry over a decade ago, joined LinkedIn on the same day that I became unemployed, and everything else that has transpired since then. However, having personal branding goes beyond creating content online and creating a persona – it's what makes you unique yet relatable to others.

I was able to tap into social media as a 'gold mine' to rebrand myself and rebuild my career thus leading me down a successful career path as a corporate marketing executive, entrepreneur and speaker. None of this happened overnight, however. Building a brand and getting to the point where others view you as influential requires time and a lot of patience. Despite having no experience in running a business at that point, I forced myself to learn how to code websites and started an online job board. Also, I had no marketing budget, so I made it a priority to learn about social media, which was relatively at ground level back then and not used by businesses in the way it is today. It was through trial and error and making a lot of noise that I discovered if you get your face and message in front of enough people some – not all – will bite.

From 2009 to the end of 2011 I was doing what we refer to today as 'social selling'. I spent the majority of my waking moments bouncing between LinkedIn, Twitter and Facebook. Every day I used LinkedIn to identify HR executives at companies where I was trying to sell my services. Then, I would go to Twitter to engage with said recruiters and executives directly. Once we were either connected via LinkedIn or following each other on Twitter, I would go to Facebook to become 'friends' so they could get to know me personally and humanize the experience. Little by little the HR industry came to know who I was – because I was everywhere.

I was able to rebrand and rebuild. Every brand, every creator and every professional has the same opportunity in front of them – to be human and relatable. Remember, it is people who buy from people. It is people who trust people. As I learned during the years that I was building my foundation and growing my business, I wasn't selling a service or a product – I was selling myself.

As you've read throughout this book, with the rise of online streaming, live video and stories, social media will continue to be a breeding ground for new creators and personal brands thus making the internet even noisier than it is today. Not only will this reality force every corporation to reevaluate their position with regard to using social media as channels for sales and marketing, but for customer care too.

As you will see in the final chapter, advances in technology including virtual reality (VR) and augmented reality (AR) will only make a human voice and face more potent than it is today. Therefore, in this new era of communication, your ability to connect with humans on a personal level will be your most effective competitive advantage.

So, how do you stand out when everyone else is doing the same thing?

Meet 'The 5Ps of Success'

'The 5Ps of Success' is a model that I began implementing early on in my career. Each trait is equally essential and all are tied to one another. Allow me to explain.

Passion

Passion is what your customers feel from you whenever they interact with or see you, whether it's in person or online. What drives you as a company or as an individual? If you're in sales, your potential customers will be able to tell quickly if you are passionate about the work you do and the company you represent. If you're an entrepreneur, your passion should be what guides you to wake up every day and run your business. Theoretically, your business should be your passion. If you work in marketing and handle copywriting for your company's social media accounts, you should be passionate about the impact that your work drives for your employer. Passion is the heart of everything we do.

Persistence

Persistence is the uncanny ability never to waver or give up on what you are striving to accomplish no matter how long it takes you to get there. During the early days of my start-up, a lot of people didn't take me seriously because I didn't have the same level of credibility and documented results that I do today. As I learned to work in the corporate world as an employee, I had to be persistent with teaching others at the companies where I worked about the value of social media. Many who work in sales and marketing give up on social media quickly because they don't see instant results. As I've covered in previous chapters, there's no immediate ROI in social media. It's a long-term play, and you have to be annoying, persistent and in people's newsfeeds to be heard or seen. Posting once and walking away just won't cut it.

Perseverance

Perseverance and persistence are similar, yet one is a mindset (perseverance) while the other is an action or tactic (being persistent). Every brand and creator begins with zero followers at the start. To build a presence on YouTube can potentially mean creating hundreds of videos before you see a significant impact, whereas platforms like Instagram and Snapchat require a mix of stunning visuals and stories that captivate people's attention. The key to 'making it' online is to look at your growth as a continuous evolution, which requires perseverance. The same can be said if you're looking at your small business Facebook page right now with less than 100 'likes' and you're asking yourself if you should continue. It's typically not a matter of if, but how. During my early years, I did a lot of A/B testing to see what worked versus what didn't and once I learned that a specific outcome could be achieved by particular tactics, I then applied those more.

Personality and persuasion

Let's face it, we are all 'in business' for the same outcome... to sell something.

As a business owner, I do very little business development or traditional sales because people know me as a result of the personal brand building and 'social selling' that I've done for over a decade now. However, someone might look at the content that I post weekly on Instagram, YouTube or LinkedIn and view my content as being my sales pitch without ever mentioning a product, service or even a website – they are correct. Through content I've humanized my brand to a point whereby I don't have to tell you what I do, you see it, and there's a level of relatability to who I am as a person when I'm not working. This is the art of personal branding, and I'm here to share the playbook with you.

From speaking to consulting opportunities, to be viewed as a trusted and credible thought leader in any industry has its benefits. However, it takes time and content to grow your influence, along with persistence and perseverance. To be viewed as an 'expert' in your field, you should have work history or experience and achieve results. Furthermore, if you're eager to begin tapping into LinkedIn and other social networks to grow your sales revenue, be ready to invest time in creating content and digitally networking with others.

The first step to growing your professional influence is to evaluate what your strengths are and what you can teach others based on your experience and results achieved.

Begin by mapping out the topics that you can teach others. For example, if someone is looking for help with growing their YouTube channel, they are likely to go to Google or YouTube and type in 'How to grow on YouTube'. Ask yourself, 'what do people want to know and what can I teach them?' then list all of the possible titles for blog and video content.

It's easy to see thought leaders such as Gary Vaynerchuk and want to emulate what they do. Sadly, it's not that easy. To grow your personal brand and influence, follow this personal brand checklist:

CHECKLIST   Personal brand

- What do your customers want to know and what can you teach them? Create a list of topics!
- Are you blogging insights and actionable tactics on Medium, LinkedIn and Facebook that your customers deem valuable?
- Are you teaching on YouTube?

AND

- Are you personally taking the time to respond on social media whenever someone engages with your content?

The secret to personal branding is to have a mix of personal and professional content. It's less about who you are as a professional and more about who you are as a person. Creating resonance means that others in your industry can relate to the content you create, yet also get value from you. If you aren't already, leverage platforms like YouTube and Instagram to share what you do for work alongside what you do for play. In my case, I have spent years letting 'digital strangers' into my home by sharing content featuring my children, what I like to do for fun and who I am outside of my day job, and at the same time I've shown them what I do professionally, as well as educate onlookers about my profession of marketing. During my early days of Snapchat, I was one of the first to market to talk about growing on Snapchat and did so within the platform. Once you become passionate about something, whatever it is, make that passion what you speak about loudly and let your personality shine through all that you do. Keep in mind that for most people social media is an escape from their everyday life. If you want to grow your influence, give your viewers or audience real and raw emotion no matter how many people are watching. Lastly, especially on Instagram, leverage your post caption to share short, intimate stories about the content that a possible viewer is seeing to make them feel connected to you and your content.

Figure 10.1 Carlos Gil on Instagram

carlosgil83

carlosgil83 Edit Profile

2,093 posts   **29.9k** followers   **305** following

Carlos Gil
AUTHOR, "THE END OF MARKETING"
PRE-ORDER ON AMAZON
endofmarketingbook.com

▦ POSTS   IGTV   ⊟ SAVED   ⊘ TAGGED

SOURCE Instagram via Carlos Gil

Figure 10.2 LinkedIn Advanced Search filters

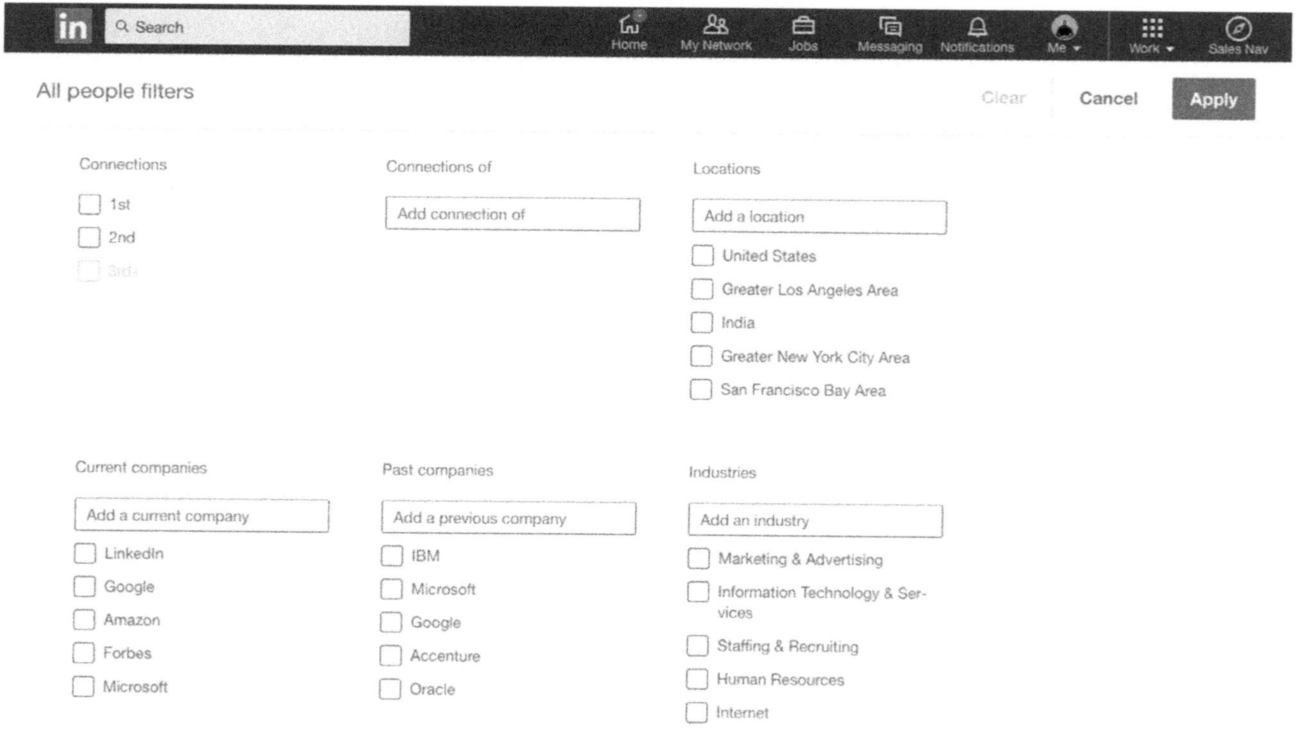

All people filters

Clear   Cancel   **Apply**

Connections

Connections of

□ 1st
□ 2nd
□ 3rd

Add connection of

Locations

Add a location

□ United States
□ Greater Los Angeles Area
□ India
□ Greater New York City Area
□ San Francisco Bay Area

Current companies

Add a current company

□ LinkedIn
□ Google
□ Amazon
□ Forbes
□ Microsoft

Past companies

Add a previous company

□ IBM
□ Microsoft
□ Google
□ Accenture
□ Oracle

Industries

Add an industry

□ Marketing & Advertising
□ Information Technology & Ser-
  vices
□ Staffing & Recruiting
□ Human Resources
□ Internet

SOURCE LinkedIn (2019)

If you work in sales or are looking to grow your business and find new clients, using LinkedIn isn't an option – it's a requirement. The good news is that LinkedIn's 500 million-plus member database is easily searchable with just a couple of clicks and completed search fields

From your LinkedIn home screen, go to the search bar in the upper top row and click on 'people'. Then, all filters. From this screen, either enter the company that you are trying to sell to or type in the job title of your ideal customer.

I own a digital marketing agency; therefore, connecting with chief marketing officers is key to growing my business. LinkedIn gives me access to reach over 21,000 chief marketing officers in the United States. However, before you Connect or send an InMail to any sales prospect, look them up on Twitter or Instagram and engage with them there before you engage on LinkedIn. The reason you should hold off on inviting a prospect to connect or send them an InMail is that most networking doesn't happen on LinkedIn, it's happening elsewhere. Plus, you do not want to appear as overly eager or spamming someone that you have yet to form a dialogue with.

A quick Google search for your prospect's name + the word 'Twitter' will reveal if they are on Twitter. If they are, see if they are active and when was the last time they tweeted. If they are on Twitter and active, send them a personalized tweet along the lines of:

> Hi (Name), I came across your profile on LinkedIn and am fond of the work you and your team at @companyusername are doing.

That's it. Don't say another word until they reply. You do not want to appear as though you are desperate or overtly selling. If they don't respond after a few days, then go back to LinkedIn and engage with them there, otherwise keep the dialogue flowing organically on Twitter until you see an opportunity to talk business offline. In some cases, you might come across an executive at a company who isn't on Twitter at all, or inactive, and you will have no choice but to engage them on LinkedIn.

There's a fine line between selling and coming across as 'spammy' on LinkedIn. Writing an InMail or any form of a message that introduces yourself and your company to a potential customer is an art form, especially when you're trying to get the attention of someone who continually receives sales pitches. Be direct but don't sell.

Before you send off an InMail that might be perceived as spam or go unread, follow these three key guidelines:

1   Do you know someone in common who can introduce you to each other? If so, ask your mutual connection to make a warm introduction, which will go further than reaching out blindly.

2   Did you recently attend an industry conference together? If so, reference the name of the conference and potentially the session where your prospect spoke, if applicable.

3   Has their company been mentioned in the news recently? If so, speak to the news headline first (this works on Twitter too!).

Professionals who run a business or manage teams are already busy and don't have time to weed through long and exhausting messages, nor are they likely to respond and agree to a message which overtly sells to them without building a relationship first. This is where you persuade them.

You will have a much better conversion rate if your InMail messages are short, direct and to the point, they reference a recent event that you attended or offer immediate value up front with a potential business opportunity. Also, clearly state how much time you are seeking from the person you're messaging.

For example, a persuasive LinkedIn InMail might read something like this:

Hi (Name),

I recently read in (industry publication) that (their company) was ranked in the Forbes list of top companies in your industry. Congratulations!

If it's okay by you, I'd like to stay in touch and will send over a connection request.

Take care,

Carlos Gil

Crafting the perfect InMail takes finesse along with a lot of A/B testing to trial what works versus what doesn't, however, keep these three must-haves in mind:

1   Be short and to the point. Within the first sentence or two, you should clearly state why you are reaching out, in addition to who you are and what you do.

2   Do not sell your company or services within the first interaction. The person that you are writing to can see your job title and your employer name on your profile.

3   Instead of suggesting getting on a conference call, begin by offering to connect on LinkedIn first.

Building a relationship on LinkedIn is no different from meeting someone offline and building a relationship organically. With over 500 million members, LinkedIn is the go-to social network for business professionals around the world. However, being discovered on LinkedIn and growing your brand as a thought leader within your industry begins with having the right combination of keywords within sections of your profile.

The first step to optimizing your LinkedIn profile is to edit the Headline section by adding industry-relevant keywords that are most likely to come up in search results or be entered in the search bar. For example, in my profile I have the keywords 'Social Media', 'Marketing', 'Consultant', 'Agency', 'Storyteller' and 'Speaker', therefore there's a high likelihood that my profile will rank high in search results if a LinkedIn user is running a search for 'Marketing Consultant' or 'Social Media Speaker' because I have a combination of these keywords in my headline.

What are your keywords? Write them down: _____

_____

As you optimize your LinkedIn profile, be sure to complete all fields including 'Education', 'Location', 'Industry' and 'Contact info', including your website, email address, phone number, Twitter account and birthday. The reason you should complete every field

Figure 10.3   How to edit the intro of your LinkedIn Profile

SOURCE LinkedIn via Carlos Gil

is that these fields are either searchable or make it easier for someone to engage with you. The more information you include, the more easily you can come up in search results.

By adding where you went to school, your profile will be indexed among the user profiles of that school or university, which improves the likelihood that fellow alumni will be able to find and connect with you. If you live in a rural or remote location, think about changing your city to the next closest metropolitan market

Figure 10.4   How to edit LinkedIn contact info

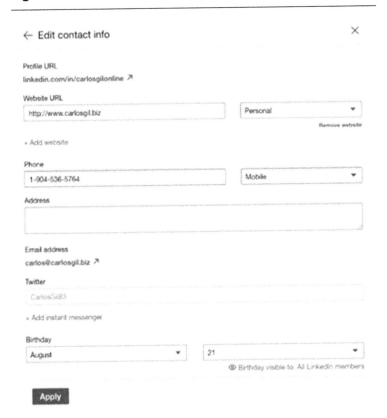

SOURCE LinkedIn via Carlos Gil

Figure 10.5 How to edit your LinkedIn contact intro

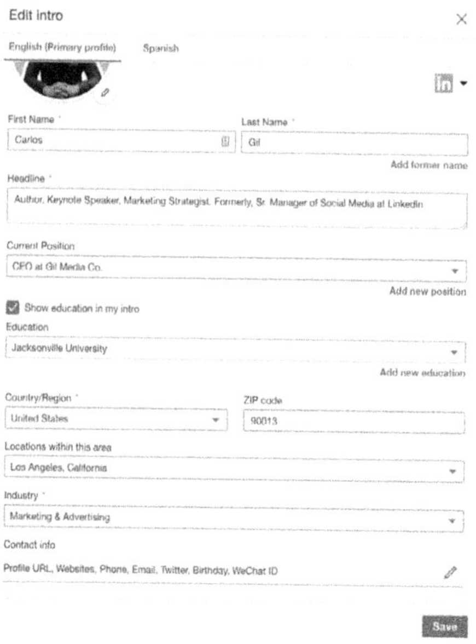

SOURCE LinkedIn via Carlos Gil

to expand your searchability. Also, select an industry that represents what you do or who you are trying to sell to. Last, add your date of birth to your profile, so on your birthday those in your network will be notified, which is an organic and free way of reaching your first-degree connections.

Your LinkedIn profile summary section is critical to being found outside of LinkedIn too, as your LinkedIn profile is typically one of the first links that pull up whenever someone runs a Google search for your name. Writing your LinkedIn profile summary is something that you should take time to master as it should read like the 'About' section of a website or the 'About the author' section of a book. The LinkedIn profile summary section should highlight your skill set, experience and what you've done throughout your career. Also, leverage this section to include relevant and searchable keywords.

Figure 10.6   How to edit your LinkedIn summary

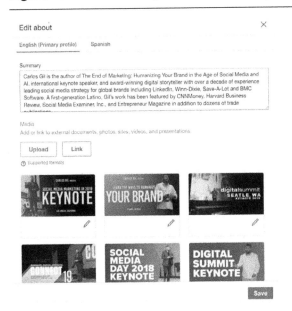

SOURCE LinkedIn via Carlos Gil

Figure 10.7   Search results for Carlos Gil via LinkedIn enhances SEO

About 23,000,000 results (0.49 seconds)

Carlos Gil - CEO - Gil Media Co. | LinkedIn
https://www.linkedin.com/in/carlosgilonline ▾
Presently, **Carlos** is the CEO and Founder of **Gil** Media Co., a **Los Angeles** based marketing firm which works with Fortune 500 clients including DocuSign, ...
You've visited this page many times. Last visit: 9/8/18

SOURCE Google

Add rich media content

Rich media content helps boost industry authority and adds credibility to your profile. If you have video content on YouTube or have been featured in trade publications, add them to your

Figure 10.8   How to add media to your LinkedIn intro

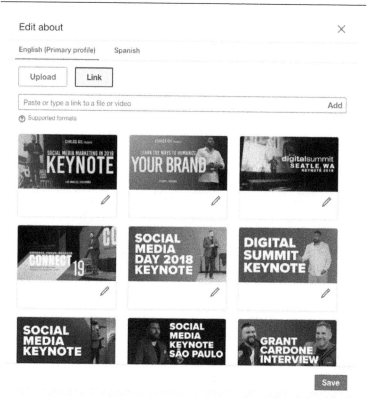

LinkedIn profile. Also, if you're in sales or B2B this is where you can add more character to your profile by adding customer success stories that live on your company website. You should also add rich media content for each one of the employers that you've listed on your profile.

What you currently do professionally, as well as where you've worked throughout your career and what you have been able to accomplish, should be reflected throughout your profile to boost your visibility and increase your professional opportunities. Your LinkedIn profile is more than a résumé; it's your portfolio and your brand.

Figure 10.9   Keyword search examples within LinkedIn

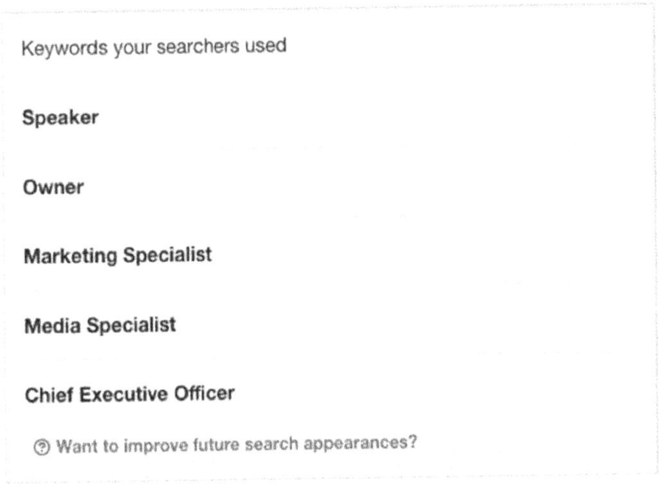

Keywords your searchers used

Speaker

Owner

Marketing Specialist

Media Specialist

Chief Executive Officer

⑦ Want to improve future search appearances?

SOURCE LinkedIn via Carlos Gil

Figure 10.10   Example of LinkedIn profile and search appearance statistics

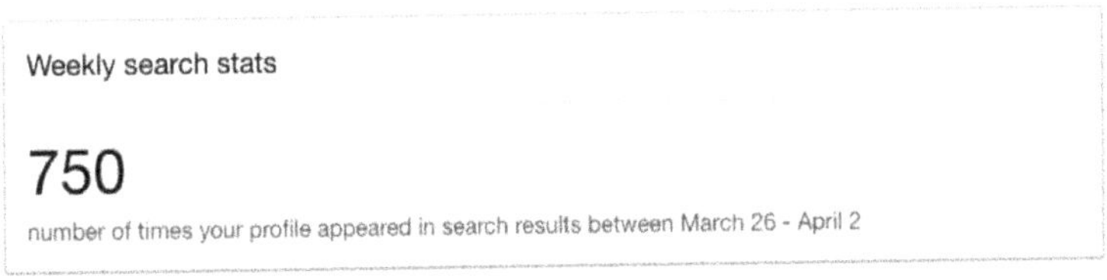

Weekly search stats

750

number of times your profile appeared in search results between March 26 - April 2

SOURCE LinkedIn via Carlos Gil

Update often and monitor

Once you optimize your LinkedIn profile, monitor your stats weekly to ensure that your profile is coming up in search results. To get the most out of LinkedIn, you need to be active on the platform, which requires contributing to discussions, posting original content of your own and joining LinkedIn Groups.

Join LinkedIn Groups

LinkedIn Groups are a quick way to expand your network. By joining an already established community of LinkedIn users, you instantly have access to potentially thousands of group members who either work in your industry, live and do business in your city, or share similar interests. Also, most Universities and schools have groups for alumni.

LinkedIn allows you to join up to 100 groups, so as best practice join as many that are relevant to you. First, go to the Work menu from your home screen followed by the Groups icon.

Once you're able to see the Groups that you are a member of, click on the Requested tab followed by Discover.

Find relevant groups

Out of 1.9 million groups, LinkedIn will recommend groups for you to join based on keywords in your profile and interests.

You can also type keywords such as 'Marketing' into the search bar to find groups for your industry. For example, when I typed in 'Marketing' it revealed over 56,000 possible groups that I could join, starting with the largest ones. You can also type in the city where you live, for example 'Los Angeles', and join groups created by the local chamber of commerce or trade association chapters that are local to where you live or do business often.

Introduce and engage

Think of every LinkedIn Group that you join as a stand-alone community within a broader ecosystem within LinkedIn. As you enter and interact within Groups, you will have your go-to groups that you'll immediately gravitate to each time you login whether it's weekly, daily or throughout your day, which is why it's critical that you introduce

Figure 10.11   How to join LinkedIn groups

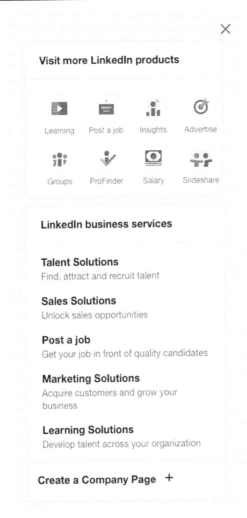

SOURCE LinkedIn via Carlos Gil

yourself upon joining. Members of the group then know that you exist and will be compelled to look you up outside of the group. Also, to grow your influence within each group, it's critical that you contribute fresh, relevant insights without self-promoting, but also engage frequently in discussions started by other group members.

By joining and actively participating in LinkedIn Groups you'll see an immediate return with more profile views, new connection requests and potentially website visits, which lead to new business opportunities, subscribers, etc. However, it's vital that you remain active and don't overwhelm yourself by joining 100 groups right away. To help you stay in the know of what's posted in the groups you're a member of, turn on email notifications so even if you aren't on LinkedIn you can be notified by email of new discussions.

When I started on LinkedIn in 2008, I was actively involved in groups for HR and talent acquisition since my business primarily focused on job placement and recruiting. By contributing to group discussions and also starting my own threads, I quickly grew my following on LinkedIn. In addition, I joined local groups for various cities outside of where I lived at the time, which helped me form relationships in other states, cities and countries that I still maintain to this day. The beauty of LinkedIn – and social media in general – is that it expands your network globally. However, the key is to contribute frequently to stay in front of people.

Create industry thought leadership

If you want to become a credible thought leader within your industry, who people trust and want to follow, it takes time and doesn't happen overnight. However, if you have hands-on experience in your field and knowledge in your craft that you can share to help others achieve measurable results in their businesses, LinkedIn has built-in tools to help you grow your thought leadership.

From Microsoft Excel to growing a YouTube channel there are experts for everything. Here's a thought leadership checklist to follow:

CHECKLIST Thought leadership

- What are you good at doing?
- What are you passionate about helping others with accomplishing?
- What are you able to teach someone?

Once you've done a self-assessment of what you're able to teach, the next step is to list a series of topics and subtopics. For example, a topic for me would be 'LinkedIn' with a subtopic being 'How to use LinkedIn Video' and 'How to Grow Your LinkedIn Connections'. The subtopics will end up being your blog and video lessons. If you can write every week, come up with a content calendar of 12–24 titles to get you through the next three to six months.

CHECKLIST Topics

- List topics and subtopics.
- Write a piece of content per subtopic.
- Create a video upload per topic.

LinkedIn Articles allows you to blog within the LinkedIn platform without having to create a stand-alone website. The advantage of blogging within LinkedIn is the SEO and organic traffic that LinkedIn receives versus striving to get visitors to go to your own hosted site or domain. The functionality that LinkedIn Articles offers is comparable to what you will find on Medium.com or WordPress, minus the technical requirements. Once you've published a blog post, it will be shared into the newsfeed and live on your LinkedIn profile too.

Create video content

To bring more visibility to your thought leadership content, create short videos that are under two minutes in length and post them natively to LinkedIn as a status update. You can make a video using the webcam on your desktop or laptop computer or using your smartphone.

Figure 10.12 How to create a blog post within LinkedIn to boost your thought leadership

Whichever method you prefer, create a short video that describes your LinkedIn article, along with one or two key takeaways from the article to motivate your audience to read it. The great thing about LinkedIn is that if someone 'likes' your content, it will appear in the newsfeeds of all their first-degree connections, which is why it's advantageous to create as much organic content on LinkedIn as possible. Also, add relevant hashtags to your post to expand your reach beyond first-degree connections.

Have a plan and be consistent

As with anything else that you do on social media, creating a recognizable brand as a thought leader takes time. However, by having a content calendar and consistently writing content, including video tutorials that live within your LinkedIn profile, you will quickly gain traction and awareness among industry colleagues. Don't forget to share your content in groups as well, for maximum viewing.

You can't post once a day and walk away

By now you're probably well aware that social media never sleeps. I refer to it as a 'giant digital ocean' for a reason, because it's not only massive, it's always on 24/7, 365 days of the year. To remain relevant and top of mind to your digital community of followers, you can't post once a day and walk away. Your content won't perform favorably and get the engagement you're seeking without checking in regularly. However, you don't always need to depend on creating new forms of content to grow your influence. Participating in LinkedIn and Facebook Groups, as well as discussion threads on Twitter and Reddit, help grow your thought leadership within an industry by merely showing up and contributing to relevant conversations. Remember, text-based posts, which we refer to as 'conversations', are content too. This is where persistence comes into practice – you MUST be 'front and center' to be seen.

Each channel requires its own strategy

Because the algorithms vary by channel and how users consume content varies, it's critical that you develop a posting strategy by channel. For example, Twitter content is displayed chronologically in real time whereas posts on Facebook and Instagram appear based on relevance and engagement.

What to do in-between posts

Assume that each post has a limited 'shelf life' with a quick expiration date. The lifeline of your posts is solely dependent on whether others are commenting or engaging with your content. Going back to my 'giant digital ocean' analogy, think of a social media post as a wave. Your wave will gain initial traction or momentum upon posting. The more that post gets engagement the more momentum your wave will attract until it reaches a peak or the highest point of consumption before it (your post) dies down and crashes to shore. The trick is to get as much engagement as possible within the first couple of hours, which means sharing your content with a hidden 'tribe' of super fans in a private Messenger or Facebook Group, sending a mass email out to your loyalty program list, or taking to Facebook or Instagram Stories to cross promote. Because of this reality, every post should be treated as a mini marketing campaign. To keep your community engaged in-between posts or upon posting, leverage tools like Instagram Stories, Facebook Stories and Twitter chats to stay 'front and center' without relying on posting fresh content every hour. Going back to humanizing your brand, begin by slowly introducing your social media team to your followers on Facebook and Instagram. Take turns by having a designated representative from your team to create content through Facebook or Instagram Stories to generate excitement upon posting a new piece of content. This tactic is a sure-fire way to make your community feel more connected to your brand. Eventually, your social media team will have their own Facebook Pages and Instagram accounts – more to come on that later.

As someone who has seen social media evolve since its early days, I can say it hasn't grown much. The only thing that has changed is the platforms but what we all want and crave remains the same – attention. Dating back to the days of AOL, and fast forward to the plethora of apps and social networks that exist today, social media has always been about people and connectivity. Somewhere corporations decided that it would be a good idea to insert themselves into pre-existing conversations without realizing that it's much easier to be part of a community than to try to be the community.

In a world where Google, YouTube, Reddit and Facebook are among the top websites visited globally, reaching your customers – and being found – is not hard. The most significant shift for marketing executives going forward will be how to take what the last decade has taught us about digital marketing and optimize traditional methods of online advertising, to put the control into the hands of the people – whether they're employees, influencers or customers – for them to relate the narrative on behalf of the company. One day we will live in an era where the face of Home Depot is a dad somewhere in Des Moines, Iowa, who shows us through social media how to do 'things' around the house, albeit through Home Depot branded channels. One thing will remain constant, however, and that's that you are only as good as your last post. Post engagement is oxygen; therefore, you should aim to post content that educates, entertains or inspires.

Here's what today's customer wants:

- People, not products.
- Faces, not logos.
- Stories, not posts.
- Experiences, not sales.

As I've reiterated throughout this book, the secret to building a loyal following on social media is sell less, engage more.

Your objective should never be to sell; it's to 'hook' your customers through your content so they will tell their friends and come back for more. That in itself is the power of personality and persuasion. Ask yourself:

- Are you likeable?
- Can you convince followers to take action?

The 'creator economy' is a big business that will only get bigger. In 2017, 17 million people in the US earned income from posting content online. By comparison, there were just about 12 million manufacturing workers in the US. And, content creators made close to $4 billion on YouTube alone (Feldman, 2019).

Part of the job is to use social media to showcase your personality or 'persona' to get people to digitally 'buy-in' and follow you. We all have a digital avatar that we play and, after establishing 'you', the second phase is to persuade people to keep coming back to engage with you.

Before you turn to the next chapter, let's connect on LinkedIn. You may find me at linkedin.com/in/carlosgilonline – but don't pitch to me or try to hard sell.

Reference

Feldman, S (2019) Where online content creators make money, 21 February [Online] https://www.statista.com/chart/17114/online-content-creation-earnings/ (archived at https://perma.cc/3GXL-3WFZ) [accessed 8 May 2019]

11
Bringing it all together

First, I want to take a moment to thank my parents, Carlos Sr and Millie Gil, for buying me my first computer for Christmas in 1996. As a shy and introverted only child, discovering the internet at a young age offered me unprecedented access to a world beyond my bedroom including the opportunity to make 'friends' and assume a level of popularity that didn't exist for me in school. So, whenever I see my kids using social media (eg, Instagram, Snapchat and TiKTok) today, it makes me realize that nothing has changed from one generation to another. We all want to be heard and seen, which is why through my lectures and keynote presentations I stress the importance of making marketing less about advertising and more about connecting on a human level. Looking back, what's ironic is that the countless hours that I spent making friends in chat rooms on America Online (AOL) set the groundwork for much of what I know today around creating an online brand, building relationships and driving business growth on platforms like LinkedIn. It's old school rules with new school tools. Meaning, since the beginning of time, relationships have always been the basis of how two parties enter into a pact. With advances in technology, all that has changed is the speed with which relationships happen.

Now that we're on the home stretch of the book, I'll start to summarize what you have learned, contextualizing this learning alongside helpful tools.

The three pillars of social media success are: BE RELEVANT. BE HUMAN. BE SOCIAL.

QUICK TIPS

- Wondering which social media networks to use? It's simple: go where your customers are. Then, be relevant by having a platform-specific strategy.

- No one wants to hear jargon and dry sales pitches. Engage with your audience to attract real customers by showcasing what makes your brand – and the people behind it – human.

- Remember why people use social media: to be social. Focus on making real connections to exponentially expand your reach.

While social media can be a potential gold mine for leads and new customers for most businesses, today's consumer has more options than ever before for where to consume and create content; therefore, it's created a noisy, digital ocean that's always on, 24/7, even when you're not working, and your business is not open. Not only are traditional brick-and-mortar businesses competing with online-based companies but they're also in a virtual competition for digital attention against everyday people, commonly referred to as 'personal brands'. In this new era of business, a company that is worth billions and publicly traded is potentially less influential on the internet than a YouTube personality like Sara Dietschy or Marques Brownlee, who are paid by brands to make them relevant.

To rise above the noise, you must first stop sounding like every other company (ie, 'Click to learn more', 'Check out this limited-time offer!' and 'Sale ends today!') and instead learn how to be more personable – digitally speaking – and human by implementing the technique of storytelling, similar to the likes of notable celebrities or internet influencers.

Your story is how customers will remember your company, and your persona is what will influence customers and help you increase brand awareness and attract new followers. Telling your brand story also requires leveraging your company's employees as storytellers to share the narrative of what happens inside your company, in addition to speaking authentically about your company without resorting to sales and marketing rhetoric. In some cases, humanizing your brand requires aligning with the influencers who are able to reach your target consumer.

CASE STUDY How shoe brand K-Swiss rebranded around the modern hustle

In its more than 50 years as a global brand, K-Swiss has undergone several transformations. From its tennis origins to its 1990s cult following, to the effective 'I Wear My K-Swiss' campaign in the early 2000s, the company has embraced rebrands to connect with customers amidst ever-changing pop culture.

Under the direction of President Barney Waters, the company began its latest pivot to become the go-to sneaker company for entrepreneurs. Since then, K-Swiss has shown an impressive ability to tap into the zeitgeist, underscored by creating a shoe line with famed marketing entrepreneur Gary Vaynerchuk. The collaboration coincided with revamped marketing efforts focused on providing valuable business insights, such as through a new K-Swiss podcast called 'CEOs Wear Sneakers'.

While other sneaker companies like Nike and Adidas battle for dominance in athletic footwear by partnering with some of the world's most famous sports stars, K-Swiss found an open lane in entrepreneurship. The company realized that young people today often aspire to create businesses, and they see grinding and hustling as a badge of honor.

To reach this audience, K-Swiss partnered with Vaynerchuk and provided value to entrepreneurs. Whether it was through conversations on social media related to building businesses or creating original content about entrepreneurship, K-Swiss formed real connections by providing practical business knowledge while inspiring people to chase their dreams.

How to hack the Facebook algorithm

Typically, Facebook only shows your posts to about 1 per cent of those who follow your page, so you need to accept the fact that engaging in paid advertising is a virtual necessity to get the most out of Facebook. Still, that doesn't mean that organic engagement can't be a part of your multifaceted marketing strategy. To reclaim organic reach, start by understanding how Facebook's algorithm works.

Types of content Facebook prefers include:

Short-form native videos

Facebook is competing head-on with YouTube in the race to be the go-to platform for digital video content, so the first type of content Facebook prefers is short-form native videos. Native means the video is uploaded directly to Facebook and plays within Facebook's newsfeed rather than linking out to another site. A big mistake that brands make is they treat Facebook like YouTube and post long videos. Yet Facebook viewers only watch an auto-play video for less than 17 seconds. As people are swiping, they're only stopping for what stands out, and even then you only have a short time in which to engage your audience.

Live video

Facebook is becoming a multimedia platform that includes live streaming, so its algorithm also shows preference to this type of content rather than a video that takes someone away from Facebook. Live video may seem complicated, but all you need is a smartphone to simply record what makes your brand human. Whether you're a B2B or B2C company, or even an individual trying to grow your personal brand, live video can be utilized by anyone to give an inside look into what you're all about. Think of the lessons from DJ Khaled and the Kardashians/Jenners and apply those to your Facebook Live video content.

Posts that ignite conversation

Since Facebook's goal is to keep people on the platform so they can ultimately deliver more ads, its algorithm prioritizes posts that get people to engage. If a post generates a lot of comments and shares, Facebook will be more likely to show that content.

To have organic reach on Facebook, it's also important to avoid pitfalls that cause your post not to be shown at all.

Avoid the following tactics on Facebook at all costs:

Overly promotional posts

If a post is overly salesy, as in it looks exactly like an ad, Facebook will not prioritize your post and could even cancel it. Their incentive is to get you to buy ads, not use their platform for free. Similarly, Facebook does not like fake news, clickbait or anything that overly incentivizes someone to leave Facebook and go to a third-party site, because again, that goes against their goals.

Long-form text

Facebook is not a blogging platform and users don't want to read long posts. Since Facebook wants to keep its users engaged, the algorithm pushes down posts that include more than a few sentences of text.

Excessively tagging others

Even though you have the ability to tag lots of people and pages in posts, don't tag more than a handful. If you tag 50 people in one post, Facebook might think your post is spam, especially if someone untags themselves from that post.

Cracking the code on Instagram

On Instagram, the content format matters less than the content quality, and the same engagement rules for Facebook generally apply to Instagram. Focus on creating content that others will want to interact with, which thereby drives up the chance that Instagram will show the post to a larger audience. Yet it's important to remember that even if posts with a lot of likes, comments and shares get shown more often, that's not necessarily true engagement that helps your brand. Real engagement requires real conversations. So, if you manage a social media account, for example, any time someone comments on your post, promptly comment back. Too often, brands view social as an opportunity to sell, not as an opportunity to actually engage in two-way conversations.

To generate genuine engagement that expands your organic reach, you need to create content that people want to respond to and share with their own networks. In addition to brands like Wendy's that do a stellar job of community management, other brands have found success by being unique, entertaining and frankly, taking a risk on being unusual. For example, a simple picture of an egg on Instagram, @world_record_egg, set the record for the most likes on Instagram with over 53 million and counting. The post is literally just a picture of an egg with a caption that speaks of beating what was then the record of 18 million likes on a post, held by Kylie Jenner.

Turn customers and employees into advocates

From active listening, you can go one step further by engaging customers and employees as brand advocates. If you pay attention to who's talking enthusiastically about your products, you can find real people who can add even more of a human element to your brand and expand your reach.

For example, if you run social media for a restaurant, there's likely plenty of people already posting photos and stories of your food on Instagram, or checking in on Foursquare and Yelp, etc. If someone shares great reviews about your brand, you can repurpose that information into new content, whether it's by retweeting them or asking them if you can use their review in other marketing materials. Reach out to these individuals, using DMs or by commenting on their posts, to connect with you further, eg, through email. You can then ask them to share more content from your brand or create new, original content, by, for example, hosting a private dinner for select customers and encouraging them to create Instagram and Snapchat Stories about the experience. This strategy is essentially a form of influencer marketing but without the million-dollar fees that major influencers rake in. Every single person is influential within their own circles, and you can tap into new networks by engaging people who already love your brand and want to spread the word. These initiatives don't have to cost you much, if any, money. Just be sure to follow applicable rules regarding ad transparency – if you're paying someone to post about your brand or providing them with something for free, they should disclose that information. If your brand has enough cachet, you might also find success by creating a unique challenge or creating buzz around product launches. Starbucks' annual release of its Pumpkin Spice Latte, for instance, prompted multitudes of social media users to share content about Starbucks on their own networks.

Similarly, you can activate your own employees to spread the word to their own networks. This strategy can be particularly powerful for B2B companies that otherwise struggle to humanize their brands. By empowering real individuals within your company to evangelize your brand, you put real faces to your company name. I've worked with several brands like Western Union to build employee advocacy programs, and I find that the most successful ones get buy-in from each of their key stakeholders. For example, if you want HR departments to get on board, you need to explain to the chief HR officer why employee advocacy can strengthen employee culture and help employees build their personal brands to advance their careers. Likewise, you need to explain to the head of sales why getting salespeople to share content leads with more eyes in the company leads to more sales. Your job as a marketer is to take every silo, make social media marketing relevant to that group, and provide each silo with content that's easy to share. From there, you can build a larger community based on real people advocating for your brand.

Have a strategy for each platform

Social media networks are not created equal. The way you create content and engage with your audience on Facebook is very different from how you do so on platforms like Snapchat or YouTube. For example, LinkedIn is generally more valuable for B2B than B2C companies, but in either case, the content should be work related. I recently posed a question on social media about whether you should hire for experience or potential, and I got way more engagement on LinkedIn than Facebook or Twitter.

Generally, you don't want to talk about work while you're on vacation, and you don't want to bring up what you had for dessert last night during a board meeting. Likewise, know what your audience expects depending on where they are within the social media universe and adjust your content accordingly. Content format also makes a difference. Even though the 63,206-character limit on Facebook is far higher than the 280-character limit on Twitter, that doesn't mean you should post essays on Facebook. Think about how users quickly scroll through their feeds. Then create content that they can realistically engage with given the confines of the platform. Keep in mind that content preferences and algorithms change over time, so it's important to stay tuned into what customers and competitors are posting and engaging with.

Most importantly, know that as a marketer, you can't have a one-size-fits-all strategy for managing your presence on social networks, and you can't repost the exact same content across each platform. The way people consume content differs on each network, and each site has a different algorithm that determines your reach.

Tools to use

To make your job easier, there's a whole ecosystem of social media tools in areas ranging from design to social listening. Some of my favorite social media tools include:

Canva

How it works: Canva is a simple design tool that allows you to create all sorts of graphics that you can customize for each social network. It uses a drag-and-drop format and provides access to over a million photographs, graphics and fonts. Although non-designers, as well as professionals, use it, think of Canva as 'Photoshop for dummies' due to its easy-to-use nature. Canva operates on a freemium basis so that you can use many of the features – such as templates – for free, but you may want to pay for more depending on your graphics needs.

Adobe Spark

How it works: Adobe Spark is also a freemium design tool, similar to Canva, but it's arguably more comprehensive than Canva. In addition to creating graphics, you can also use it to create videos to use on social media. Download the Adobe Spark iOs or Android app and get started in seconds with professionally designed templates you can tweak with just a few taps. Pick your photos, add text and apply Design Filters to create beautiful, eye-catching graphics instantly. Remember, it's all about 'show don't sell'.

Buffer

How it works: Buffer serves primarily as a freemium social media scheduling tool, where you can load posts in advance and automatically publish them on your selected time and date. Since you want to be human, you don't want to use only scheduled posts. However, it can be an excellent addition to your social media toolbox, as scheduling posts can save time and keep you organized, for instance, if you have a planned product launch announcement or even just a video that you're planning to release on a particular day. Buffer also has a variety of design and analytics capabilities that you can take advantage of.

Hootsuite

How it works: Like Canva versus Adobe Spark, Buffer also has competitors such as Hootsuite that allow you to schedule posts and analyze your social media traffic. Poke around these platforms' websites and take advantage of free trials to see which one is best for your brand.

Sprout Social

How it works: Sprout Social is a comprehensive social media marketing tool that's similar to Hootsuite and Buffer but is much more feature rich, with social listening capabilities that help you keep track of what customers are talking about across social media. Unlike the tools listed above, Sprout Social does not offer a free version of its platform other than a free trial.

Mailchimp

How it works: While not technically a social media tool, Mailchimp or other email marketing platforms should also be a part of your social media marketing strategy. As I have said through this book, your job as a marketer is to capture customers' data. Once you create connections on social media and start to collect their email addresses, use platforms like Mailchimp as a low-cost customer relationship management (CRM) tool. You can segment your customers into different lists, from which you can then send out engaging emails to keep the conversations going, away from social media.

TubeBuddy

How it works: TubeBuddy is a Google Chrome plug-in, which has both free and premium versions. You can download TubeBuddy at tubebuddy.com/carlos to trial its features. With TubeBuddy you can get over a dozen tools and features that are critical for growing your YouTube channel, including recommendations on what tags to insert into your videos as well as the ability to see how your videos rank in search results.

FAQs

Moving on from tools, below are the most frequently asked questions that I hear whenever I speak at a conference or present virtually via webinar, some of which you might be asking yourself while reading this book.

Do I have to be on every social network?

Answer: No.

Here's why: as tempting as it is to increase your visibility by jumping on every social network, it's a lot of work to take on. Instead of creating accounts just for the sake of having a profile, be purposeful with the social networks you choose. That means instead of joining a newer social network like Vero or TikTok for the purpose of being early, tap into existing communities on Instagram and YouTube instead. While you can't be everywhere and be effective, you should aim to be on the social networks where your customers are, where you can get the most significant reach. An easy way to figure out which social networks to be on is by simply asking where your audience's attention is. If they're not on Pinterest, there's no need to spend a bunch of time and energy there.

Another good test for which networks to choose is by asking yourself what value you can bring to the network. If you can't create content that people on the network want to see, put your efforts elsewhere. If you have the time and resources to make outstanding videos, then you should have a presence on YouTube so you can share those videos across the networks your audience love most. If you don't have the bandwidth for video production, get off YouTube and don't feel guilty about not being there.

Which is better for my business: Snapchat or Instagram?

Answer: Instagram.

Here's why: Snapchat and Instagram are both popular among a wide range of audiences, including Millennials and Generation Z. Initially, the primary differentiator was that on Snapchat, unlike Instagram, the photos and videos you send are only visible for a few seconds before they disappear for ever. Then Instagram came out with its version of 'snaps' through Instagram Stories. While both can be advantageous for your marketing strategy, they also require a significant commitment of time since the visual content is shared as disappearing, short stories. Because they disappear, it's more work to have to constantly create content to stay relevant. However, just because you can advertise on a platform doesn't mean that you should. Especially if your marketing department is small or you have limited capacity.

Critical differences between Snapchat and Instagram should be considered before allocating your marketing dollars. One of the key benefits to using Instagram is that your content doesn't disappear, so it can be found organically by users who type in the hashtags you're using. Plus, you can link to your website on your profile. Snapchat is another story. While there is a Discover function, it is not nearly as user friendly as Instagram's Search & Explore and due to the temporary nature of Snapchat stories, the depth and breadth of content aren't there. So based on this, Instagram is the clear winner.

Do my usernames have to be consistent?

Answer: Yes.

Here's why: not only will it be easier for you to promote your social media handles if they're consistent, but it will also be easier for fans to find and tag you. When usernames are different across every network, it can get confusing. If you tweet an Instagram image, but you have two different usernames, it complicates things. Inevitably, someone will tag your Twitter name on Instagram or your Instagram name on Twitter, and you'll miss opportunities for engagement.

Today it's not only domain names that matter; usernames are just as, if not more, valuable in terms of digital real estate considering that your username appears in the URL of your profile address. What's more important is that your usernames are consistent across each network. One of my biggest regrets is not securing @CarlosGil everywhere. Instead, I'm @CarlosGil83 on Twitter and Instagram but have varying URLs on LinkedIn, Facebook and YouTube.

What type of content should I share?

Answer: The type of content your audience wants to see.

Here's why: it all comes down to knowing your ideal customer. If you have a solid understanding of their lifestyle, desires and pain points, it will become much easier to create or find relevant content they're likely to enjoy and share. Beyond that, follow influencers in your industry who produce excellent content and share their stuff.

You can also search relevant hashtags or check out what's trending on Twitter and Instagram to understand what people are talking about right now, then join in on those conversations. Idea generation is the hardest part, so let your audience do it for you. Talk to your followers or ideal customers and ask them what they would like to see. You can also ask your employees to contribute one blog post per month. When you divvy up the work, it becomes less stressful and more thoughtful.

How do I get more followers?

Answer: You don't need more followers. You need more buyers.

Here's why: regardless of which network you're talking about, it's the quality, not the number of followers that matters. You need followers who will engage with your content, not just add to your follower count. Therefore, don't worry about how many followers you have – it's only a vanity metric.

Instead, be more concerned about growing buyers and loyal brand advocates. Since people are bombarded with content from all over the place, you have to give them a compelling enough reason to follow you. You're not just asking people to follow you.

You're asking for their attention, which is a limited resource. Why should they give their attention to you instead of someone else?

How do I get organic reach on Facebook?

Answer: Keep Facebook users on Facebook.

Here's why: Facebook has openly said that its algorithm favors content posted from personal profiles and not brand or company pages. Today less than 1 per cent of your page followers actively see content posted by your company in their newsfeed, arguably making Facebook a 'pay to play' platform for brands. Here's what you can do to reclaim organic reach on Facebook without paying to reach your fans:

CHECKLIST   Organic reach on Facebook

- Post content directly to Facebook – known as native posting – versus using a third-party scheduling tool.

- Keep traffic contained on Facebook instead of attempting to send users to your website or YouTube. If you are posting website links in your content, there's a high likelihood that the algorithm will deprioritize your content.

- Use Facebook Live to host a weekly show from your company account or tap into Facebook Live for product demos. By using Facebook Live, Facebook will send a notification to your followers as soon as you go live.

- As an alternative to posting links that point users to your company blog, try using Facebook Notes.

- Create a group for your most engaged fans or one that's relevant to your industry.

How can I hack the Facebook algorithm?

Answer: Engage on old posts.

Here's why: if a Facebook user goes through an extended period without engaging with your business page content or they don't intentionally visit your page, it's likely they will never see your content again unless you pay to run an ad or a friend in their network engages with your business page content.

As best practice, you should respond to all comments and reviews left on your business page within 24 hours; however, it's possible that throughout the years you've ignored opportunities to engage your followers. By engaging within the comments section of any old Facebook post on your business page, you will 'trick' the Facebook algorithm into thinking your post is new and relevant. Facebook will also notify users who previously commented on your post content.

To re-engage missing fans from your Facebook business page, follow these steps:

1 Go to reviews left by customers on your business page and respond to all of them. By commenting on a review, even if it's outdated, the customer will be notified by Facebook, which is likely to trigger them to visit your page.

2 Leveraging Facebook Page Insights, identify your best-performing posts over the last year. 'Like' and reply to every user who commented on your posts. Doing this will trigger Facebook to notify those users and also resurface the post into the newsfeed as if it were new.

3 Last, run Facebook Ads targeting fans who have 'liked' or engaged with your content within the last 12 months. To do this, you will need to create a custom audience.

I'm new to YouTube, where do I begin?

Answer: What are you able to teach?

Here's why: on the surface, one might look at YouTube as a place to watch music videos, stream video games online and tune in to one's favorite vlogger. However, as the second most-searched site online, YouTube is an untapped gold mine for businesses and creators.

Having an active presence on YouTube can help you gain precious website visits and drive leads as a result of the videos that you post. As an added benefit, your YouTube videos are also discoverable via Google search. Because Google owns YouTube, you have a higher likelihood of being discovered through a video related to your topic or subject matter expertise that you upload to YouTube than a traditional Google search, which crawls the entire internet.

To grow your first 10,000 subscribers, follow this checklist:

CHECKLIST   Growing your subscribers

- In 2014, while working a full-time job, I started my channel to vlog my life and gave up after not seeing a significant number of views. It wasn't until I began to record social media how-to, tutorial style, videos like the ones you see today that my purpose became clear. So, what's your purpose for being on YouTube?

- To get video views and subsequent subscriptions on your channel, you should research what else exists in the same genre or category. My process for creating videos on YouTube involves writing out the titles of topics that I am passionate about teaching and then researching both Google and YouTube to see what currently exists and what the top-ranking titles are.

- You will need to ensure that your videos have keywords as tags to improve discoverability. With TubeBuddy you can get recommendations on what tags to insert into your videos as well as see how your videos rank in search results for set tags.

- What are you able to teach that people are running a Google or YouTube search for (eg, 'How to do …')? There are two reasons why people go on YouTube: to be entertained or to be educated.

- The most common objections that I hear from business professionals who want to dive into YouTube to create but don't, are access to equipment, lack of expertise in editing and time. If you run a small business and need content, consider hiring a freelancer who can shoot and edit, and bring that person in every week.

Should I use hashtags?

Answer: Yes and no.

Here's why: although social media hashtags were initially exclusive to Twitter, today all content on Twitter is searchable based on keywords in tweets. Similarly, Facebook crawls keywords in posts. Therefore, hashtags are not required. However, on a social network like LinkedIn or Instagram, adding hashtags to your posts that are relevant to your content will increase the likelihood that a non-follower will see your content. To maximize your reach, you can try adding hashtags of trending topics to your content; however, be careful that you don't spam a feed with content that isn't relevant or applicable.

When writing a social media post for LinkedIn or a post caption on Instagram, be mindful of how your use of hashtags will appear to the eyes of an end user. You do not want hashtags to take away from your message, which is why I recommend that you post hashtags in the comments section of your Instagram post, and on LinkedIn only use one or two hashtags suggested by LinkedIn as needed.

Why should my employees become better storytellers?

Answer: They make your company real and relatable.

Here's why: social media storytelling is a newer form of content marketing made popular by Snapchat and Instagram, as well as YouTube personalities. While consumers have grown tired of seeing content that appears to be an advertisement from a brand or corporation, storytelling is a tactic for individuals and corporations to be viewed as being 'real' and 'relatable' without relying on professionally produced content. With stories, think of your employees as the stars of your own reality series.

The key to telling good stories on social media is less about the platform and more about the story that you're trying to convey. Because stories typically expire within 24 hours of being posted, they should be short, attention-grabbing, and drive users to take a specific action. As best practice, you should storyboard your content whenever possible to have a beginning, middle and end.

Possible storytelling ideas for a corporation or business can revolve around the launch of a new product whereby storytelling is used to record a product demo; employees often do 'day in the life' takeovers on their company Snapchat or Instagram accounts; and stories can also be used by influencers who are compensated for taking over your brand account.

Is Facebook dying?

Answer: No.

Here's why: Facebook is still the leading social network among consumers with over 2 billion active users, followed by Instagram with 1 billion. In the last several years, Facebook – which owns Instagram – has made many feature updates and enhancements to its Stories, Live Video and Facebook Watch toolset to empower its users to improve the quality of native storytelling within the platforms. And, to compete with YouTube as a go-to destination for consuming video content. Facebook is one of the most influential companies in the world. It's not going anywhere.

I'm in a 'boring' industry, do I still need social media?

Answer: Yes.

Here's why: social media isn't just for athletes, celebrities, influencers and well-known brands. When it comes to marketing, your goal is to reach your target audience where they're paying the most attention. And for the past 10+ years, that has been social media. A whopping 78 per cent of Americans have at least one social media profile, so there's a strong chance your target customers are on at least one of the major networks.

Remember, social media isn't an advertising platform for you to shout your message as loudly as possible. Instead, use it as a platform to educate and entertain your audience. For instance, taxes are about as dull as it gets for most non-accounting people. But H&R Block puts together fun social media campaigns that don't make you cringe at the thought of tax season.

Does influencer marketing work?

Answer: Yes, but it has its flaws.

Here's why: influencer marketing is already a billion-dollar industry and will continue to grow as an alternative to traditional print and TV media advertising, which is typically more expensive. However, the state of influencer marketing is significantly flawed. When you take several factors into account, such as influencers buying fake followers and buying engagement, one can view it as an ineffective method of marketing. Instead, companies should create their influencers.

An influencer doesn't need to be internet famous to be influential. An influencer can be an existing customer who already speaks about you organically without compensation or it can even be an employee. Whoever you deem to be influential, engage them directly to endorse your company or services through written testimonials on their blog and social media accounts, or have them create a YouTube review in the form of a video.

How can I work with brands?

Answer: Engage them directly.

Here's why: if you want to work with brands and get sponsored you have to go to them directly and pitch to them on what your potential value is to them. My advice is never to lead in with your follower count, because as I've shared throughout the book, renting an audience is a temporary solution to a bigger problem. Instead what you need to do is sell them on the content that you would like to propose creating for them. Brands don't need your followers; they need your content.

The two easiest platforms to pitch brands directly on are Instagram and Twitter, by sending a direct message (DM). Within the DM, mention that you'd like to 'collaborate' with the brand and want to know if they 'partner' with influencers and creators. By using words such as 'collaborate' and 'partner' you are making your pitch more personal and inviting. Also, begin by engaging brands that you already purchase products from.

What's the biggest 'secret' that no one else is telling me?

Answer: You're only as good as your last post.

Here's why: it's the same on any social network: you are only as good as your last tweet or post. A social media post has a relatively short lifespan and is only relevant as long as it has engagement. Engagement on posts is a form of oxygen; therefore, you should always aim to post content that delivers value through education or entertainment to your intended audience.

Above all, be social

While tools can help you elevate your content and engage with your audience, the key to success in social media is to always remain true to the purpose of social networks. Be social, be real, and you'll be able to make waves in this digital ocean.

Have a question that's not answered here? Tweet me your question to @CarlosGil83 and I will answer it for you. Remember, there's no such thing as a dumb question, so ask away!

12
The new frontier

When I set out to write this book, I knew that I wanted to write something different from the thousands of social media self-help books already out there. I wanted this to be not just a book, but a map to guide the modern-day marketer in his or her quest to grow their digital relevance. While I could have written a book teaching anyone the basics of building a personal brand or an entry-level guide to social media marketing years ago, the timing didn't feel right as I still had to grow personally and professionally.

Having evolved from a start-up entrepreneur to a marketing executive that's worked for corporations such as LinkedIn has given me valuable hands-on experience and great perspective as it pertains to the business of social media marketing.

However, it is my passion for being a student that enables me to thrive as a practitioner – one cannot be an expert or guru in a space that's continually evolving unless he or she grows themselves. In an era where a business using social media for marketing purposes was once new, I've had the privilege of learning directly from those who paved the path before me, such as Seth Godin, Brian Solis, Jay Baer and Gary Vaynerchuk. Not only have I benefited by learning from their teachings, which I've applied throughout my career, but from them I know that a book should offer a fresh perspective and vision of where the world is headed. It's about being a trailblazer.

The premise of *The End of Marketing* is for your company to survive. Leading up to 2030 you will need to build a human-centric business that's *less* about your logo, products and services and *more* about the people who make your business run – your customers and employees. While the theory of having a digital presence where your customers are and being human isn't a new concept in business, replacing your digital brand identity altogether with a face *is*.

In fact, this applies to how this book came about. I learned about Kogan Page through a social media post and was introduced to the editors by Michael Brito (who is a fellow Kogan Page author and wrote *Participation Marketing: Unleashing employees to participate and become brand storytellers*). Despite not having pitched this project to any other publisher beforehand, I asked Michael – over Facebook Messenger nonetheless, and in-between conversation related to my beloved Jacksonville Jaguars – if he could kindly make a warm introduction to his publisher. The point here is the value of relationships. Had it not been for Michael's introduction I may never have written this book.

Like Michael's willingness to help me, we are all a by-product of the people that we meet, relationships developed and experiences encountered. One fantastic experience between a brand and customer can lead to the said customer becoming the company's most prominent advocate because they (the company) showed digital empathy and listened. Likewise, showcasing your employees as the faces of your company shows that you have formed trust by empowering them to engage on your behalf. To the outside world this establishes that you care and have created a workplace where people are valued.

I am passionate about humanization as a business strategy because I've lived it and have built an entire career around it. Case in point, according to Re:Create Coalition's study 'Where online content creators make money', in 2017, 17 million people in the US earned income from posting content online, and YouTube creators made close to $4 billion – an increase of 20 per cent year on year. By comparison, there were only 12 million manufacturing workers in the US during this time (Feldman, 2019). The creator economy alone is a big business within an even broader industry, which are the social networks directly disguised as digital advertising media.

Unless you, as a business, come to terms with the fact that your competition is no longer only your fellow corporations, but you're also competing against real human faces, your business will eventually cease to be relevant or possibly exist altogether.

Evolve or die

If you want to know what the future holds, look at the previous decade for insights. The world permanently changed when the late Steve Jobs and Apple released the iPhone in 2007, followed by the App Store in 2008. Our dependency on technology and instant accessibility has grown stronger ever since. For example, the Sony Walkman that I used in the 1990s is now built in to my iPhone. I have an extensive library of songs through Apple Music or Spotify, versus relying on driving to a mall, parking, and walking to a music store to buy a CD with one or two good songs and a dozen useless tracks. Poor Kodak, once a billion-dollar company in existence for over 130 years, went from dominating the photographic film and camera industry during most of the 20th century to going bankrupt due to the rise of smartphones with high-definition cameras. Photography went from being a skilled profession or hobby that one would do for fun, to being something that we all do to document or journal publicly.

For Baby Boomers and Millennials, the advent of the iPhone has made life more accessible than it was before. Meanwhile for Generation Z or those born after the year 2000, it's all they know. Outside of having 24/7, unlimited access to the internet in our pocket, the iPhone gives us the ability to consume digital content (ie, music, movies and connectivity) on a mobile device whenever we want. How much are you using your mobile phone these days to text and make phone calls compared to using social media?

A quick view at my Screen Time within the Settings menu of my iPhone shows that I spend on average 5 hours and 26 minutes on my phone which is nearly one-quarter of a 24-hour day.

Figure 12.1   Screen time data

When you factor in the time that I spend on my iPhone every week, it equates to almost 2,190 hours spent on my phone, or 91 full days. That's one-quarter of the year occupied by an iPhone and the technology within it.

In a sense, we are 'digitally enslaved'. Once you become dependent on forms of technology to operate, you are a slave to the technology and cannot exist without it. Without Facebook or Instagram, many would lose their identities altogether. In many ways, we have become digitally enslaved human robots and when you factor in social media, we've become citizen journalists too. However, understanding this paradigm shift in how we are evolving as humans will ultimately make you a better business operator.

How to continue to engage new audiences

Once you come to terms with the paradigm shift social media has brought about in the last decade, it doesn't stop there. For your business to continue to evolve alongside humanity, you need to constantly keep an eye on what's coming – and stay ahead of the curve, or at least on it. Three technologies to monitor for engaging new audiences are: **voice, virtual and augmented reality**.

Apple's Siri, Amazon's Alexa and Google Assistant are becoming more common every day in our lives. Eventually, you will be able to do everything from order groceries through Alexa – which is connected to your Amazon Prime account – to listen to your favorite podcasts by asking Siri for recommendations. Personalization will increasingly become integral to the role that your company plays in the lives of consumers, which is why building meaningful relationships (quality over quantity) starting now will be more pivotal than the number of followers you have on social media. Also, as voice marketing gains awareness, having a podcast that is hosted by your company will give you another distribution medium to reach potential customers in their home or office without them having to rely on learning about you through social media or visiting your website.

Moving on to virtual reality (VR) and augmented reality (AR), these two technologies serve different purposes. Virtual reality functions by blocking out the physical world and transporting the user to a simulated world. Augmented reality, on the other hand, adds virtual information to the physical world, meaning the user perceives both worlds.

According to a study by the Global Agenda Council on the Future of Software & Society (World Economic Forum, 2015), it's estimated by 2030 these technologies will speed up the merger of physical and digital identities. Augmented reality will be used as a learning tool, to improve the training of individuals. Virtual reality will make it possible for users to immerse themselves in alternative scenarios, thus serving as a preparation for future situations.

Facebook – which owns Oculus VR, one of the largest creators of virtual reality hardware and software – already has 'Facebook Spaces', which is a fully immersive experience to interact with your Facebook friends in virtual reality. I'm going to play conspiracy theorist for a moment and suggest that since the advent of the iPhone we have been conditioned to consume content on a mobile device, with the goal being first to get us used to relying on a device for content consumption. What happens, however, when the device is no longer the main point of entry, and we can either access the internet – and social media – without a phone or we're able to be 'inside' the internet and hang out with our friends, wearing a headset? It's not a matter of if but when it happens, which is why I suggest that you don't write off Facebook. We've yet to see what Facebook's plan for world domination entails.

One of the early pioneers of augmented reality is Snapchat, through its popular face filters and lenses. Snap, Inc. – parent company to Snapchat – which calls itself a 'camera company' allows you to convert your iPhone camera lens into an AR projector while you're inside the Snapchat app. To date, dozens of high-profile brands including Kay Jewelers and CoverGirl have leveraged Snapchat's AR capabilities to allow users to try on jewellery and make-up, meanwhile McDonald's and Bud Light have used Snapchat's AR features to engage Snapchat's younger demographic to incorporate product placement into 'snaps'.

While advances in technology will continue to make the world a more connected ecosystem, to 'future proof' your business for a 2030 society you must focus on **people and platforms**.

Millennials and the C-suite

Here's a thought to ponder: Millennials will soon be C-level executives at most corporations, and it's likely we will have a Millennial President of the United States by or around 2030. It's estimated that by 2030 the Millennial generation will have 78 million people whereas the Baby Boomer generation will have only 56 million people in the United States, thus increasing the buying capacity of Millennials (Statista, 2019). Also, over the next decade Generation Z will be the most significant spending generation of all time. This passage is a long way of saying if your company plans to remain in business over the next decade, you must find a way to get in front of Millennials, as well as Generation Z, and build relationships with them. However, to forge relationships with two demographics that have grown up with social media means you must be flawless on the networks and bring purpose to their lives rather than deliberately trying to advertise to them. For example, look at an event like Coachella, or SXSW, that's highly popular among both demographics and ask yourself: what can my company do to reach this audience? It's not limited to just pushing out tweets with relevant hashtags but rather having a physical presence at festivals, concerts and events through things like pop-up experiences. This demographic will feel compelled to share their experience with your brand with their friends through social media.

In the future, marketing will be less about pushing out content from brand channels and more about consumers marketing on behalf of the company with branded content (eg, sponsored GIFs, photo booth activations and videos from experiences). Customers who feel compelled to share your branded content will be the stars of your marketing campaigns.

The platforms

As people evolve, including Millennials and Generation Z, so will the platforms. While Facebook and YouTube won't suffer the same fate as AOL and MySpace once did, how we use them will change. Eventually, Facebook and YouTube will replace cable television providers. YouTube, which is owned by Google, already has its YouTube TV streaming service, which has all of the network channels you'd find on a cable TV provider. Expect Facebook Watch to become a stand-alone network with original programming including series and shows (see, eg, Amazon Prime and Netflix), but made by internet creators, which will be the key differentiator to rival YouTubeTV. In the long term, both Facebook and YouTube will be more about *media* than social networking.

So where does that leave you and your company? Start planting the seeds to create a weekly series through Facebook Stories and Live. Pay attention to the 'template' of video creator pages already on Facebook – or sign up to Facebook for Creators – to see all of the built-in features that Facebook offers, which allows a bit of foreshadowing for what the future holds. If you have an e-commerce business or can sell products and services direct-to-consumer currently, Facebook has a robust set of features in place today to allow you to run your DTC business from your Facebook page, including integration with Shopify, which removes the friction of converting ads to website visits or leads. Expect 'social commerce' to be more relevant over the next decade, whereby your Facebook business page acts as a digital storefront in which customers can purchase, leave real-time reviews and rate your brand similarly to leaving a Yelp review. Although it's not a social network (yet), it wouldn't be surprising to see Amazon rival Facebook with social commerce and add social networking features into the Amazon Prime suite of media and services.

Final thoughts

Will Facebook continue to be free?

Answer: No.

Here's why: there are two reasons why Facebook continues to be 'free', the first being that since its inception, Facebook has been in growth mode to acquire users. Because there's no associated cost with joining, Facebook users don't have any barrier to participation besides the minimum age limit – they have to be at least 13 years old. The second is that they can sell data to third parties, including brand advertisers. With over 2 billion monthly users, Facebook reportedly made $40.65 billion in 2017 with $39.94 billion coming from advertising revenue (Dreyfuss, 2019). According to an article by Recode, as of 2017 mobile ad spend is higher than desktop ads and will only continue to skyrocket as more individuals get access to smartphones (Molla, 2019).

In the same article, Recode also reveals that in 2019 the average individual consumed 400 daily minutes of content, with television gaining the most significant market share at 164 minutes and mobile internet at 122. Eventually, Facebook will hit a ceiling and its growth will slow down, no thanks to already existing concerns around privacy since the Cambridge Analytica breach came to light. Expect Facebook to eventually have a premium subscription service to make up for potential lost ad revenue, while also creating a new P&L line item for subscriptions from millions of members who wish to opt out of ads in their newsfeeds, similarly to how Spotify and Pandora have premium and free versions of their services.

While Facebook and YouTube will reign supreme over the next decade, it's likely we will see a consolidation of social networks, including brands cutting back on the number of social media profiles, as well as fewer social media start-ups and more new apps that act as utilities to integrate with Facebook, Messenger, WhatsApp and even Slack. As far as what will happen to Snap Inc., parent company to Snapchat, it will be acquired by either The Walt Disney Company because of its appeal to younger audiences, or NBCUniversal in an attempt to transform Comcast into a mobile-based microcontent network. As far as Twitter goes, it wouldn't be surprising to see it acquired by a tech giant like IBM yet see no change by consumers, much how Microsoft acquired LinkedIn. And yes – a decade from now we will still be unable to edit tweets.

What emerging social networks are worth keeping an eye on? Answer: TikTok, Twitch and Reddit.

Here's why: eventually, younger consumers (ie, Generation Z) will 'grow up' just like Millennials, who once were early adopters of AOL, MySpace and Facebook, did. However, should your company rush to jump onto TikTok, Twitch or Reddit right now? The answer is no. If you don't have an immediate business need or you are not trying to reach this audience just yet, wait to see how these platforms evolve.

The social network that I would spend the most time getting to know – because it's not really 'new' – is Reddit. Reddit, which was founded in 2005, is a news aggregation, web content rating and discussion website – similar to the 'old school' message boards of the 1990s. It's also one of the most visited websites online. Registered members submit content to the site such as links, text posts and images, which are then voted up or down by other members. To be candid, if leveraged properly it can be a phenomenal source for driving website clicks, email opt-ins, and subscribers. However, here's the catch – the Reddit community is anti-marketing therefore participating in Reddit discussions should resemble the dialogue of an everyday person, not a brand (albeit that's what this entire book has told you already). To grow your presence on Reddit begins by engaging in community discussions related to your industry or topics relevant to your customers. It's social listening 101.

Twitch is the next most promising social network that I would investigate. Owned by Amazon, Twitch is a live-streaming video platform with 81.5 per cent of its users being male and 55 per cent ranging between the ages of 18 and 34 years old (Twitch, 2019). Although Twitch doesn't boast the same size user base as the likes of Facebook or even Snapchat with approximately 15 million daily active users, its users spend on average 95 minutes per day consuming streaming video content, primarily video games, due to the rising popularity of Fortnite and Esports. If you're looking to get into YouTube at the ground level, look no further than Twitch. From Totino's Pizza Rolls sponsoring the first-ever 'Bucking Couch

Bowl' during Super Bowl 50 – a tournament between top Twitch players – to gamers plugging brand sponsors such as Taco Bell at the very beginning of their broadcasts, Twitch is an influencer's paradise and yours too.

TikTok is worth eyeing, but I'd recommend proceeding with caution here unless your target demographic is between the ages of 13 and 18 years old. Formerly known as Musical.ly, TikTok, also known as Douyin in China, is an iOS and Android media app for creating and sharing short videos. The application allows users to create short music videos of 3–15 seconds and short looping videos of 3–60 seconds. It is a leading quick video platform in Asia, the United States and other parts of the world, with an estimated 500 million active monthly users. The reason why I am skeptical about TikTok is that we have seen this before – it was called 'Vine' and it was acquired, then killed off by Twitter. While TikTok is highly addictive for younger demographics, for brands to appeal to this audience they require either a tremendous amount of talent, which as we've already addressed is naturally lacking, or the resources to hire TikTok influencers to shout them out through product placement.

The new marketing department

Along with a renewed focus on how we use social media to grow market share and competitive share of voice will come important new performance indicators. While historically brand marketers have reported KPIs such as 'impressions' to go along with 'follower growth' and 'engagements', we will need to report on more advanced metrics such as 'return on engagement (ROE)', which measures new revenue generated based on a set number of engagements with a user, whether they're a first-time or returning customer. The number of direct engagements it takes to get a customer to buy will be an accurate measurement of how many touchpoints it takes to get a customer to buy. Also, get used to adding 'customer relevance score' to how you value your community, including those speaking about you and your competition, based on the number of times a user mentions your brand, your competition or your industry. The roles within a marketing department are likely to change as well, with the chief digital officer (CDO) being the new chief marketing officer (CMO) owning everything from social media, website, email marketing and digital advertising, as traditional advertising (ie, print, TV/radio, et al) becomes obsolete. Key marketing roles over the next decade will focus on analysing data and programming AI to perform tasks once completed by a social media community manager. Let's not forget that marketing departments will also hire in-house storytellers and content creators.

As companies get on board with making employees the faces of their brands, look for the CDO to be at the helm of most organizations as a 'public figure' and pseudo chief communications officer.

Create your influencers

Today, 'The Shorty Awards' have become the social media influencer's version of The Grammys and The Oscars. The business of influencer marketing will continue to grow, which will force companies to rethink what they look for when hiring creative and marketing talent. Eventually the world's largest brands will begin to poach talent straight from Snapchat and Facebook's public-facing lists of preferred creators and retain these individuals as full-time creative directors and chief engagement officers (ie, 'the new CEOs'), to brand their organizations' content as having the same fun, creative nature that the influencers portray on their own channels. On the flip side, you will have companies like Adobe, which has formed deep relationships with over 60 B2B thought leaders and influencers as part of their #AdobeInsiders program to act as journalists on behalf of the organization at industry conferences. The #AdobeInsiders program is a model of excellence for other brands to follow and shows both the depth and width – of attention – a single brand can drive by recruiting influencers who reach various age, racial and gender demographics.

Speaking of influencers and the business of influencer marketing, let's not forget that Facebook and YouTube will eventually begin to groom their own breed of homegrown talent – if they aren't already – and then offer them 'for rent' directly to brands, cutting out the middle man being the everyday content creator or influencer marketing agency.

Conversational marketing

Predicting the future can be a fun exercise. Over the next decade, we are likely to see everything from fully autonomous self-driving cars, next-generation displays such as implants, and cryptocurrency possibly replacing printed money, a Millennial as President of the United States, 3D-printed houses and meals, clothing connected to the internet and AI as CEOs. One social media trend that will grow mainly due to the rise of AI and bots will be conversational marketing. Through conversational marketing using programed AI and bots, marketers will be able to have always-on, real-time conversations with customers from beginning to end of the buyer's journey. Imagine a world in which you don't have to write yourself a reminder to follow up with a client or send a carefully crafted LinkedIn InMail, and whenever your client has a question, they can write to your AI, which will have a perfectly curated message waiting. Once a company like IBM acquires Twitter, they will have nearly two decades' worth of conversational data points for machine learning to identify sales opportunities and start conversations well before a human can.

Conclusion

It's always been about the customer, not technology, and it always will be. The main reason why businesses fail is not because they weren't first to Facebook or were unable to adapt quickly to advances in technology, but because they weren't able to meet their customer's needs before their customer went somewhere else.

Regardless of what products you sell or industry you represent, we are all in 'the people business'. People buy from people. People trust people. What technology offers every online business is the ability to get in front of potential customers before your competition does, and quicker than relying on the old methods of yesteryear that are no longer useful.

So, the easiest way to 'future proof' your business is to be where your customers are. From there, it's all about the experience. The relationship that you develop with your customers should be unique on a case-by-case basis. Building loyalty and advocacy doesn't happen at scale, it happens little by little in the direct messages (DM) in the late evenings when your customer is upset at your company, or at the weekends when your staff has gone home to rest, yet your customer is inside one of your stores.

In an always-on, AI-dominated world, the last frontier of true independence is our brain and our thoughts. Like dating, if you can convince another human being that they are heard and valued so that they will then, in turn, tell all of their friends about you, then you've won. As humans, we will always need to feel wanted, appreciated and connected. That's far from marketing; it's psychology.

While marketing, as we know it, *is* dead the need to sell and grow revenue will never die. If cash flow is the life support of a business, engagement through social media is its oxygen.

In closing, all that social media networks are is distribution media. Use them wisely. You own your brand regardless of what medium you chose to broadcast on, but the key is to **own your data** – and remember that the network you're playing on is a ticking time bomb that could go off at any time without notice.

References

Dreyfuss, E (2019) Facebook changes its ad tech to stop discrimination, *Wired*, 19 March [Online] https://www.wired.com/story/facebook-advertising-discrimination-settlement/ (archived at https://perma.cc/Z6CT-KY2U) [accessed 13 May 2019]

Feldman, S (2019) Where online content creators make money, *Statista*, 21 February [Online] https://www.statista.com/chart/17114/online-content-creation-earnings/ (archived at https://perma.cc/3GXL-3WFZ) [accessed 13 May 2019]

Molla, R (2017) How Apple's iPhone changed the world: 10 years in 10 charts, *Recode*, 26 June [Online] https://www.vox.com/2017/6/26/15821652/iphone-apple-10-year-anniversary-launch-mobile-stats-smart-phone-steve-jobs (archived at https://perma.cc/BV46-26YE) [accessed 13 May 2019]

Statista (2019) Number of people in the United States in 2011 and 2030, by generation (in millions) [Online] https://www.statista.com/statistics/281697/us-population-by-generation/ (archived at https://perma.cc/K4RU-KTDM) [accessed 13 May 2019]

Twitch (2019) Twitch audience [Online] https://twitchadvertising.tv/audience/ (archived at https://perma.cc/M2PH-GMWZ) [accessed 13 May 2019]

World Economic Forum (2015) Deep shift technology: Tripping points and social impact, survey report, September [Online] http://www3.weforum.org/docs/WEF_GAC15_Technological_Tipping_Points_report_2015.pdf (archived at https://perma.cc/2ZQW-NLWP) [accessed 21 June 2019]

INDEX

A/B testing 58, 94, 162, 169
Adams, Gerard 78
Adidas 9, 187
Adobe 29, 216–17
Adobe Spark 193
#AdobeInsiders program 216–17
advertising 58–59, 213
  see also Facebook Ads
advocates (advocacy) 30, 125–42, 157,
  197, 206, 218
  employee 10, 24, 67, 83–84, 115,
    120, 190–91, 201–02
  Instagram 120–21, 190–91
AI (artificial intelligence) 143–57, 217
Alexa 209
'All I Do Is Win' 118–19
Amazon 4, 17, 38, 145, 209, 212, 214
Amazon Prime 209, 212
ambassadors 114, 115, 120–21
American Airlines 85, 156
Anderson, Tyler 57, 83–84
AOL (America Online) 7, 33–34,
  54, 185
App Store 207
Apple 207, 209
  see also iPhone; iTunes
Apple Music 207
apps 80, 147, 155–56, 183, 213
Armstrong, Mario 79
audience 8–9, 64–65
  targeting (customers) 22, 23–26,
    30–31
audit, Facebook pages 67–69
augmented reality (AR) 209–10
authenticity 115, 117, 127, 187
auto-commenting 151–55
auto-likes 151–57
auto-reply bots 66, 151–54
Ayala, Shaun 137–39

Baby Boomers 6, 207, 211
Baer, Jay 205
Balvin, J 155

Bambu 134, 135
'BeSocial' 133, 134, 135, 136
Best Buy 138, 139
Beta testing (groups) 134, 136
Beyoncé 11
Black Friday 48, 116
Blake, Roberto 86
blogs 60, 67, 82, 103, 120, 121, 141,
  179–80, 197
BMC Software 61, 77, 99, 133,
  134–35, 136, 140
'bot fail' 148
bot farming 151
bots 66, 105–07, 145–54, 217
brand ambassadors 114, 115, 120–21
brand mentions 40–42
  see also @mentions
brand reviews 45, 199
brands 3–4, 5, 6, 7, 9, 25, 35, 40–42,
  203–04
  personal 12, 35–36, 71, 75–77, 98,
    101, 127, 137, 159–84, 186–87
  and social media 11–15, 19–20
Brito, Michael 206
Brownlee, Marques 186
B2B 24, 60–61, 174, 191, 216
  see also BMC Software
'Bucking Couch Bowl' 214–15
Bud Light 210
Budweiser 125
Buffer 135, 193, 194
Burson, Brandon 130

calls to action 62, 81, 83, 97–98, 123
Cambridge Analytica data
  scandal 57, 213
campaigns 2, 7, 10, 57, 126, 135, 157
  see also K-Swiss
Canva 67, 193
Captain Phillips 38, 46
captions 65, 67, 82, 139
Cardone, Grant 150
CareerBuilder 94

Castaway 23, 46
celebrating success 118
celebrities 1, 2, 3, 11, 109–24, 126,
    130, 140
    see also Balvin, J; DJ Khaled;
    Kardashian West, Kim;
    personalities
'CEOs Wear Sneakers' 187
Chatfuel 145, 150, 153
cheap engagement 21
cheat code strategy 92
cheating 89, 90, 91–92
chief digital officers (CDOs) 216
chief engagement officers 216
Cicero, Nick 56
Ciroc Vodka 114, 118
Cleaner 105
clickbait 62, 189
ClickFunnels 94
Clinton, Hillary 10
CNNMoney 96
Coachella 155, 211
Coca-Cola 3, 6, 11, 56, 117, 125
Cole Haan 120–21
comments 59, 66–67
community management 39, 145, 190
company perception strategies
    46–51
competitor analysis 27–29
competitor brand mentions 41–44
competitor social media ads 45–46
competitor trolling 48
consistency 119, 181, 196–97
Constant Contact 95
consumerism 4, 6
content 23, 66–67, 197
    user-generated 83–84
    visual 80–81, 85
content analysis 26–29
content calendars 181
content creation 57, 72–73, 78, 79,
    115, 120, 122
    Facebook 58–67, 182, 192
    Instagram 22, 27, 29, 82, 182,
        189–90
    posts 103–04
    Snapchat 87, 120, 137–39, 140,
        162, 201
    YouTube 184
    see also captions; posts

content hubs 136
conversational marketing 217
conversations 181, 189
corporate communications 133, 136
CoverGirl 210
creator economy 184, 206
cross-promotion (cross-posting) 4, 69,
    122, 140, 182
custom audiences 64–65
customer advocates 190–91
customer relevance score 215–16
customers 10, 67, 120, 157, 217–18
    targeting 22, 23–26, 30–31, 64–65

data access 96
data ownership 218
Design Filters 193
Diageo 114
Dietschy, Sara 73, 186
digital enslavement 208–09
digital pirates 29
digital savagery 29, 40–51
digital speak 35
Discover (Messenger) 147, 176
Discover (Snapchat) 196
DJ Khaled 112–15, 117, 118–19, 123
DM (direct message) 13, 22, 26, 31,
    34, 105, 106, 191, 203, 218
DocuSign 61, 138
Domino's (bot) 148–50
Douyin *see* TikTok
Dr. Dre 6
Drake 6, 116
Dynamic Signal 134

Elevate 134, 135
Ellevest 50–51
email 34, 61, 94, 95–96, 133, 150,
    182, 194
email lists 64–65
email newsletters 69
email notifications 102, 178
emojis
    Domino's 148, 149
    Taco Bell 48, 49
employee advocacy 10, 24, 67, 83–84,
    115, 120, 128–42, 190–91,
    201–02
employee retention 131, 132
employee surveys 136

engagement 3, 8–9, 13–15, 19–23, 25–
    31, 59, 83, 117, 203–04, 215
    between posts 182–84
    competitor social media ads 45–46
    old posts 63–64, 198–99
engagement bait posts 62
engagement bomb posts 22
engagement pods 104–05, 110
Esports 214
executive leadership team 132, 136
Express Wi-Fi 17

Facebook 7, 8, 11, 17–18, 24, 25–26,
    27, 53–70, 188–89, 202
    Adobe 29
    bots 145, 146
    content format 182, 192
    engagement 198–99
    future use of 211–13
    Giphy 48
    growing talent 217
    organic reach 198
    Pink Slip Parties 96–98
    see also 'Hire Carlos' Facebook
        page; Messenger; WhatsApp
Facebook Ads 10, 28, 40, 64–65, 117,
    199
Facebook algorithm 58–61
Facebook for Creators 212
Facebook Groups 58–59, 65, 69,
    100–01, 181, 182, 198
Facebook Live 18, 61, 68–69, 188,
    198, 202, 212
Facebook Notes 60, 62, 67, 82, 103,
    198
Facebook Page Insights 199
Facebook Spaces 210
Facebook Stories 182, 202, 212
Facebook Watch 60, 202, 212
Facebook Watch Party 102–03
fail fast approach (trial and error) 89,
    92, 93, 94, 160
fake engagement 150–51
fake followers 92, 150–51, 203
fake news 62, 189
Fantasy Wrestling Federation
    (FWF) 34
FAQs 137
fear of missing out (FOMO) 2
F8 Conference 17–18

5Ps of success 161–73
following (followers) 91–92, 151,
    197–98
Fortnite 3–4, 214
Foursquare 190

Galant, Greg 72, 114
Generation X 6
Generation Z 6, 34, 47, 71, 196, 207,
    211, 214
ghost accounts 105
GIFs 48, 138, 154, 211
Gil, Carlos Sr 185
Gil, Millie 185
Gil Media Co 26–27, 61
Giphy 48, 50
Godin, Seth 205
Gomez, Selena 11
Google 25–26, 57, 101, 144, 163, 167,
    172, 183, 200, 212
Google Analytics 137
Google Assistant 209
Google Chrome 194
Grande, Ariana 11
growth hacking 63–66, 89–90,
    92–107

handles, social media 196–97
Hanks, Tom 23, 38, 46
hard metrics 91
hashtags (#) 41, 42, 117, 181,
    197, 201
haters see trolls (trolling)
Headline section (LinkedIn)
    169–70
'Hire Carlos' Facebook page 74
Home Depot 183
Hootsuite 40, 135, 194
Hostess Snacks 48
'How I Found a Job in an Uber' 75
'How to Prepare for a Job
    Interview' 75
HR departments 137
Hulk Hogan 33, 38
Hulkamaniacs 38
Hulu 17

'I Wear My K-Swiss' 187
Indeed.com 94
industry mentions 44

influencers (influencer marketing) 5,
    6–7, 9–16, 25–26, 109–10,
    115–16, 191, 203, 216–17
    see also celebrities; micro-
    influencers; personalities
InMail 167, 168–69, 217
InMyFeelingsChallenge 1, 116
Instagram 8, 9, 11, 24, 80, 117, 155,
    196–97, 202
    advocates 120–21, 127, 129, 132,
        190–91
    bots 105–07
    and brands 4, 5, 7, 203
    content creation 22, 27, 29, 82,
        182, 189–90
    DMs 203
    engagement pods 104–05
    and Facebook 58, 64
    Giphy 48
    growing subscriber base 90, 162,
        164–65, 167, 182
    hashtags (#) 116, 201
    Kardashian West, Kim 111, 112,
        118–19
    share groups 22
    storytelling 81, 201–02
    voice messages 156
    see also Instagram Stories; Miquela,
        Lil
Instagram pods 104–05
Instagram Stories 1, 67, 78, 87, 111,
    114, 122, 155, 182, 196
Instant Messenger 34
International House of Pancakes
    (IHOP) 44, 47
internet access 2, 17
Intuit 114
iPhones 17, 207–08, 210
iTunes 1, 9

James, LeBron 114
Jenner, Kylie 11, 190
Jobs, Steve 207
JobsDirectUSA 54, 93–98

K-Swiss 114, 187
Kaepernick, Colin 126
Kardashian, Kourtney 112
Kardashian West, Kim 11, 111–12,
    115–16, 118–19, 143

Kay Jewelers 210
*Keeping Up With The
    Kardashians* 110, 111
keyword search examples,
    LinkedIn 175
Khaled, Khaled Mohamed *see* DJ
    Khaled
@KickSpotting 120
Kodak 207
KPIs 68, 99, 110, 131, 137, 215
Krawcheck, Sallie 50

'land grab' 77
leadership *see* executive leadership
    team
likeability 87, 184
likes 59, 66–67, 90–91, 92, 151–57,
    181
Lil Miquela 155
LinkedIn 24, 54, 74, 75–77, 93–94,
    99, 120, 155, 166–75, 192
    acquired by Microsoft 213
    hashtags 201
    native blogging 103
    video content 179–81
    see also Elevate; InMail; LinkedIn
        Articles; LinkedIn Groups;
        LinkedIn Sales Navigator
LinkedIn Advanced Search filters 166
LinkedIn Articles 82, 179, 181
LinkedIn contact information 171–72
LinkedIn Groups 94–95, 101–02,
    176–78
LinkedIn profile 169–71, 174–75
LinkedIn profile summary 172–73
LinkedIn Sales Navigator 102
Live (Facebook) 1 8, 61, 68–69, 188,
    198, 202, 212
live videos 60–61, 160, 188
long-form text posts (content) 62–63,
    82, 122, 189
Lopez, Tai 30, 117
Lush 128

machine learning 143, 144, 145, 146,
    148, 217
Mailchimp 194
ManageFlitter 105
ManyChat 145, 150, 153
marketability 86, 87, 116

marketing departments 215–16
Marriott 147–48, 150
McDonald's 4, 28, 48, 210
Medium 67, 82, 103, 179
@mentions 41, 42, 43, 44
Messenger 6, 17, 66, 74, 105–06,
    147–48, 150–54, 156, 182, 213
Messi, Lionel 11
metrics 56, 90–91, 197, 215–16
micro-influencers 4
Microsoft 178, 213
Millennials 6, 8, 71, 75, 113, 196, 207,
    211, 214
Minkoff, Rebecca 127
Miquela, Lil 155
mobile messaging apps 80, 147,
    155–56, 183, 213
monitoring statistics 175
Monster.com 94
MoonPie 48
music industry 9
Musical.ly see TikTok
MySpace 7, 54, 57, 86–87, 127,
    212, 214

National Geographic 11, 80
native blogging 103
native posting 135, 198
native video content 29, 60, 64,
    67, 188
NBCUniversal 213
Neistat, Casey 114
net promoter score 45
Netflix 17, 212
New World Order 36
Nike 3, 6, 11, 80, 114, 125–26, 131,
    141, 187
Nintendo 7, 92
notifications 61, 74, 90, 102, 150,
    178, 198

objectives 119
Oculus VR 18, 210
Open Broadcaster Software 61
open-ended questions 59, 83, 104
organic reach 198

Palmer's Cocoa Butter 114
Pandora 213
passion 161

Patagonia 80
Paul, Jake 33, 117
Paul, Logan 117
PepsiCo 4, 56
perseverance 162
persistence 162, 181
personal brand checklist 164
personal brands 12, 35–36, 71, 75–77,
    98, 101, 127, 137, 159–84,
    186–87
personalities 36, 201
    see also celebrities
personality 159–84
personalization 156, 209
persuasion 159–84
pilots 136
Pink Slip Parties 96–98
Pinterest 195
platform reliance 78–79
Pop-Tarts 48–49
posts 103–04, 189, 204
    engagement bait 62
    engagement bomb 22
    engaging in-between 182–84
    engaging with old posts 63–64,
        198–99
    long-form text 62–63, 82, 122, 189
    native 135, 198
predictive analytics 144–45, 146
Prime 209, 212
pro-wrestling 33–36, 38–39
promotion 30–31, 61–62, 189
Publix 4 3, 45

questions 21
    open-ended 59, 83, 104
    screener 101

Real Talk 72, 73, 79, 90, 93,
    114, 127
Real World 110
reality TV 2, 110–11
Reddit 80, 130, 181, 183, 214
References 8–9
relationship building 25, 38, 75,
    85–86, 146
relevance 117, 182
@reply 41
Rev.com 65
reviews 45, 199

rich media content 173–75
Rock, The 11
Ronaldo, Cristiano 11

sales (selling) focus 118, 122
Samsung 11, 114
Savage, Randy 38–40
'savagery' 29, 40–51
Save-A-Lot 45, 99
Screen Time 207–08
screener questions 101
Search & Explore (Instagram) 196
search queries 48–49
Sega Genesis 92
shadow banned 151
sharing stories 122, 123
Shiggy 116
Shopify 4, 8, 60, 212
'Shorty Awards' 216
Silk 114
single sign-on 135
Siri 209
Snap Inc. 210, 213
SnapChat 8, 9, 38, 72, 73–78, 155,
    162, 196, 210, 214
    content creation 87, 120, 137–39,
        140, 162, 201
    DJ Khaled 112–15
    growing subscriber base 164
SnapChat Stories 73, 77, 122,
    191, 196
Snoop Dogg 6
social commerce 212
social media 2–8, 10, 12–13, 22–23,
    36–38, 109–24, 128, 186, 195,
    201–02
    and brands 11–15, 19–20
    and company perception 46–51
    consolidation of 213
    strategy 192–95
    see also Facebook; Instagram;
        LinkedIn; Snapchat; social
        media handles; Social Media
        Marketing World; Social Media
        Masterminds Group; social
        selling; TikTok; Tinder;
        Twitch; Twitter; YouTube
social media bots 145–57
social media handles 196–97
Social Media Marketing World 79

Social Media Masterminds Group 21,
    57, 59
social media success 116–19
social selling 160
SocialOomph 106
soft metrics 91
Solis, Brian 205
Sony Walkman 7, 207
spamming 26, 63, 167, 201
Spotify 1, 9, 38, 207, 213
Sprinklr 134
Sprout Social 27, 40, 134, 194
stakeholder benefits 132
Starbucks 43, 125, 129–30, 131,
    140, 191
Stories (Facebook) 182, 202, 212
storyboarding 81–82, 121
storytelling 34–35, 77, 81, 117–18,
    119–24, 126, 139–40,
    201–02
strategy 46–51, 92, 192–95
success, celebrating 118
Super Bowl 56, 215
Swift, Taylor 6, 11
SXSW 211

Taco Bell 47–48, 49, 50, 215
tagging 63, 189
target customers (audience) 22, 23–26,
    30–31, 64–65
Tencent 147
Terminator 2: Judgement Day 144
Tesco Mobile 47
@TheFiloDapper 120
'There's No Quit in Hustle!' 75
third-party partners 64
thought leadership 178–79, 180, 181
TikTok 8, 38, 185, 195, 215
Tinder 80, 84–85, 86
Totino's Pizza Rolls 214–15
ToysRUs 7
travel industry 10
trial and error (fail fast) 89, 92, 93,
    94, 160
trolls (trolling) 47, 48
Trump, Donald 10
trust 131, 206, 218
TubeBuddy 194–95, 200
Turbo Tax 114
Twitch 8, 38, 214–15

Twitter 24, 27, 48, 87, 96–97, 99, 111, 117, 155, 167
  bots 146
  content format 182, 192
  DMs 22, 203
  future of 213
  verified checkmarks 91
  and Vine 38
  see also ManageFlitter; Twitter pods
Twitter pods 104–05

unfollowing 151
Unicorn Frappuccino 130, 140
UrbanDictionary.com 47
user-generated content 83–84
usernames 41, 196–97
Utton, Nick 90–91, 93, 134, 136

value 86, 195
value-tainment 21
vanity metrics 56, 91, 197
Vaynerchuk, Gary 37–38, 75, 114, 163, 187, 205
verified checkmarks 91
Vero 195
vertical video 67
video captions 65, 67
video content 179–81
  native 29, 60, 64, 67, 188
  vertical 67
  see also Facebook Live; live videos; YouTube; YouTube personalities
view counts 28, 72, 77–78, 103
Vine 38, 215
virtual reality (VR) 18, 209–10
visual content 80–81, 85
vlogs 68, 72, 74, 75, 77, 81, 111, 199–200
voice messages 156
voice technology 209

Wade, Dwyane 126
Walmart 116, 129
Walt Disney Company 213

Watch Party sharing 102–03
Waters, Barney 187
WCW 33
webinars 137, 195
WeChat 147
Weight Watchers 114
Weiner, Jeff 99
Wendy's 28, 44, 47, 190
West, Kanye 9, 111, 112
Western Union 132, 191
WhatsApp 17, 147, 213
'Wilson' (volleyball) 23
Whole Foods 6
Winn-Dixie 43, 45, 55–56, 98–99
Winn-Dixie Carlos (@WinnDixieCarlos) 55
WordPress 103, 179
@world_record_egg 11, 190
Wright, Travis 74
WWE (World Wrestling Entertainment) 35
  see also WWF
WWF 33, 35, 36
WWF *Superstars* 33

Ye (West) 9
Yeezys 9
Yelp 35, 190, 212
YouTube 25–26, 74–77, 80, 81, 87, 147, 155, 184
  and Facebook 59–60
  future use of 211–12, 213, 217
  growing subscriber base 162, 163, 164, 195, 199–201
  'In My Feelings' views 116
  Starbucks training videos 129–30
YouTube personalities (creators) 1, 19, 37, 59, 71–72, 184, 206
  see also Blake, Roberto; Brownlee, Marques; Dietschy, Sara; Neistat, Casey
YouTubeTV 212

Zuckerberg, Mark 7, 18, 54, 57

CPSIA information can be obtained
at www.ICGtesting.com
Printed in the USA
BVHW061050011019
559796BV00001B/1/P